TEACHING SECONDARY ENGLISH

General Editor: Peter King

Teaching A level English Literature: a student-centred approach

Also in this series

TEACHING A LEVEL ENGLISH LITERATURE: A STUDENT-CENTRED APPROACH

JOHN BROWN AND TERRY GIFFORD

ROUTLEDGE

First published in 1989 by
Routledge
11 New Fetter Lane, London
EC4P 4EE

Printed in Great Britain

British Library Cataloguing in
Publication Data

Brown, John, 1934–
   Teaching A Level English
literature : a student-centred
approach.—(Teaching secondary
English).
1. Secondary schools.
Curriculum subjects:
English literature
I. Title II. Gifford, Terry,
1946–
III. Series
820' .7' 12

ISBN 0-415-01641-X
ISBN 0-415-01642-8 Pbk

To all our students, past and present

CONTENTS

GENERAL EDITOR'S PREFACE

Over many decades English has been a central subject in the secondary school curriculum, a position confirmed by the proposals for a national curriculum contained within the 1988 Education Act. Parents and employers, pupils and teachers appear to accept this centrality and would probably agree with these confident words which come from a statement about the function of English in the curriculum made by the D.E.S. in 1981:

> English is of vital importance in the development of pupils as individuals and as members of society: our language is our principal means of making sense of our experience and communication with others. The teaching of English is concerned with the essential skills of speech, reading and writing, and with literature. Schools will doubtless continue to give them high priority.
>
> (*The School Curriculum*, D.E.S., 1981)

Such confidence belies the fact that there has been, and continues to be, much debate among practitioners as to exactly what constitutes English. The desired consensus remains altogether uncertain, despite the framework suggested by a national core curriculum and the introduction of grade criteria to indicate the levels of understanding and skills demanded in the curriculum for GCSE English. But at least the interested teacher now has a large and useful literature on which he or she

can profitably reflect in the attempt to answer the question
'What is English?' There have been notable books designed to
re-orientate teachers' thinking about the subject from the
pioneering and somewhat evangelical *Growth Through English*
by John Dixon (1975) to the more recent publications arising
from important research into the development of writing
abilities which include *The Quality of Writing* (1986), by
Andrew Wilkinson.

Although it is essential for the English teacher to understand
and appreciate the nature of theoretical and research study
supporting the subject, what he or she most needs at the present
time is help to increase awareness of curriculum possibilities
and to reflect upon day to day classroom experience. During the
1980s a number of books have provided help for English
teachers to get a purchase on their daily activities – books like
David Jackson's *Continuity in Secondary English* (1983), which
attempts to sketch a developmental framework for English 11–
16, and Robert Protherough's *Developing Response to Fiction*
(1983) concerned with creating space for exploring pupils'
response to books. While new ideas for teaching English are
always welcome a teacher's confidence is not so much built
from making 'everything new' as much as from learning to
combine the best from the older traditions with some of those
newer ideas. And preferably these ideas have to be seen to have
emerged from effective classroom teaching. The English
teacher's aims have to be continually reworked in the light of
new experience, and the assurance necessary to manage this is
bred out of the convictions of other experienced practitioners.
This is of particular importance to the new and inexperienced
teacher. It is to such teachers and student teachers that this
series is primarily directed.

The books in this series are intended to give practical
guidance in the various areas of the English curriculum. Each
area is treated in a separate volume in order to gain the necessary space in which to discuss it at some length. The aim of the
series is twofold: to describe good practice by exploring the
approaches and activities reflected in the daily work of an
English teacher in the comprehensive school; and to give a
practical lead to teachers who wish to try out for themselves a
wider repertoire of teaching skills and ways of organizing syllabuses and lessons. Taken as a whole, the series does not press
upon the reader a ready-made philosophy, but attempts to

provide a map of the English teaching landscape in which the separate volumes highlight an individual feature of that terrain, representing its particular characteristics while reminding us of the continuity between these differing elements in the overall topography.

The series addresses itself to the 11–16 age range with an additional volume on sixth-form work, and assumes a mixed ability grouping, at least in the first two years of schooling. Each volume begins with a discussion of the problems and rationale of its chosen aspect of English and goes on to describe practical ways in which the teachers can organize their syllabus and lessons to achieve their intended goals, and ends with a brief guide to books, resources, etc. The individual volumes are written by experienced teachers with a particular interest in their chosen area and the ideas they express have been proved by them or their colleagues in their own classrooms.

It is at the level of the practical that any synthesis of the various approaches to English can be gained, and to accomplish this every teacher must be in possession of a rationale and an awareness of good methods wherever and however they have been achieved. By reading the books in this series it is to be hoped that teachers will be encouraged to try out for themselves ideas found effective by their colleagues, so gaining the confidence to make their own informed choice and planning in their own classrooms.

Peter King
May 1988

ACKNOWLEDGEMENTS

To help students gain confidence in their development as readers and writers has been our main intention in writing this book. We can assure readers that all of the practical suggestions, designed with an eye on their learning potential, have been tried out with groups of students in various classrooms over a number of years. We have received help and advice from many friends, colleagues, and students, and would like to take this opportunity to thank them all publicly. Any shortcomings in the book are ours, not theirs. As teachers, we are both now working with older students but we are continuing to experiment and adapt ideas and approaches which we first used with our own A level students. We would welcome reports from any teachers who are trying out new approaches or who decide to adopt some of the suggestions which appear later in the book. Education and learning are all about collaboration and sharing, and being vigilant for what students are ready for at any particular stage.

We want to express our special thanks to our very efficient typist, Joyce Henderson.

John Brown and Terry Gifford
(Bretton Hall College of Higher Education)

The authors and publishers would also like to thank the following for permission to use copyright material:

Faber and Faber Limited for permission to reprint extracts from 'The Other Side', from *Wintering Out* by Seamus Heaney; 'The Love Song of Alfred J. Prufrock' and 'Preludes' from *Collected Poems 1909–1962* by T.S. Eliot; 'Wind' from 'The Hawk in the Rain', 'View of a Pig', 'Esther's Tomcat', 'Hawk Roosting', 'Thrushes', 'Snowdrop', 'The Jaguar', and 'Pike' by Ted Hughes; William Heinemann Limited for permission to quote from *Waterland* by Graham Swift; the English Centre for permission to reproduce extracts from 'The English Magazine'; and Peter Daw for permission to use material from an article of his in 'English in Education' published by NATE Publications.

1

INTRODUCTION

With innovation and development in every other aspect of the
English curriculum, A level English Literature, in its orthodox
forms, is unique in surviving virtually unchanged for over two
generations. A 1933 Higher School Certificate paper in our
possession contains questions which a student of tomorrow
would find familiar. For example:

> Distinguish between the melancholy of Shelley and that of
> Keats.
>
> (6 July 1933)

Some teachers welcome this stability and wish to preserve traditional approaches to the study of literature which were
established in the first half of this century. Others find its
conservatism frustrating, and are bewildered that a course
which represents the pinnacle of English studies in school
remains unaffected by recent developments in critical theory.
There are pioneering groups eager to deconstruct A level and
offer radical alternatives.

We hope that this book will be useful to both groups: while
the bulk of the text describes practical ways of helping students
to become advanced active learners, we also attempt to re-
examine the aims and objectives of A level in the light of critical
theory. Although the examination boards may continue to
ignore the public debates about literature, criticism, culture,
politics, and education, there are now clear signs that changes

at A level will become unavoidable. Already there are flourish-ing alternative syllabuses (see Chapter 8), which allow enter-prising teachers to experiment and challenge the orthodoxy (see Peim 1986; Goddard 1985). Now that coursework has been officially endorsed by GCSE, the traditional A level final examination will become an anachronism, providing no sense of continuity with the new courses at 16-plus. There have been changes, too, in the clientele.

Designed originally as a preparation for university aspirants, A level now has to cater for a new generation of students, many of whom claim quite different interests and expectations. With vastly increased numbers of entries (from just over 9,000 in 1952 to over 60,000 in the 1980s), A level English Literature now has a majority of students who have no intention of pur-suing English into higher education. Are teachers and examiners confident that the divergent interests of all those who study A level will be met by syllabuses which reflect so little innovation? We shall try to offer practical solutions to this problem by concentrating on the student as reader, learner, and writer.

In our preparation for this book we have been helped by many A level students, both past and present, who have talked openly about their expectations, likes, and dislikes. Some are already book addicts when they join the course and enjoy reporting on the pleasures of reading; others, in contrast, are not great readers, become daunted by what they perceive as difficult and remote set books, and come to rely heavily on teachers and critics. We know readers with a huge appetite for books: one girl read the six major novels of Hardy as well as Gissing's two-volume biography in six weeks. A few students confessed to having little curiosity about words and language, while others complained about doses of dictated notes and packaged information. Many expressed enjoyment of group discussions and some were genuinely surprised and pleased by how much they learnt from their peers. Some students are keen to take part in workshops and presentations from day one, while others are hesitant readers, reluctant to join in public renderings. Such a range of attitudes and abilities presents a great challenge to teachers when planning the course, and they get little enlightenment from the examination boards, who appear to be divided on many basic issues.

In brief, there seems to be no agreed policy for deciding which texts should be compulsory (apart from Shakespeare), nor on the total number of books to be studied, nor on the time allowed for answering each question, nor on the relevance of recently published literature. The annual crop of set books is the only thing resembling a syllabus and often it is not easy to discern a coherent policy of selection. (This makes the concept of AS Literature ludicrous, as there is no unifying coherence in the present A levels.) At best there is a random list of books judged to be worth studying, although many seem chosen without real thought to the age and sensibilities of young adults.

When we turn to public statements of aims and objectives we find most of the boards are rather economical, but a few are more explicit and helpful. JMB states:

> The JMB recognises that the aim of a sixth-form English course is to present the subject as a discipline that is humane (concerned with values), historical (setting literary works within the context of their age) and communicative (concerned, that is, with the integrity of language as a means of enabling human beings to convey their thoughts and feelings to another).

This has the makings of an interesting course which would reveal the problems of studying literature. 'Humane' and 'values' reminds us that A level is in the tradition from Arnold and Leavis, but we would want to consider, with students, how texts have been valued differently by certain social and academic groups. Some critics have overstated the ideological determinism reflected in art and underestimated the originality of the artist, but an assertion like the following is a good starting-point for exploring the concept of value:

> The problem of value is the problem of the social production of value . . . . Value is not something which the text has or possesses. It is not an attribute of the text; it is something that is produced for the text.
>
> (Bennett 1979)

One consequence of this first aim is the exclusion of popular literature because of its dubious value, or of books that are so recent that there is no academic consensus as to their value.

The second aim, to set a book in its historic context, is a familiar one on any advanced course of reading, and yet, too, this is inherently problematic. Whichever accounts of a period of history we refer to we will encounter bias; nor can we easily escape our own presuppositions and predilections. It will therefore be important for students to be introduced to conflicting interpretations of history so that they may become more aware of the problems of understanding both the past and the present:

> To explain the past to the present means not only coping with shifting perceptions, values and languages, but also with developments after the period under review.
>
> (Lowenthal 1985)

The third aim, concerning the 'communicative' elements in literature, introduces a further series of problems. Can we so easily talk about the 'integrity' of language when all kinds of discourses try in different ways to manipulate us as readers? By helping students to recognize the power of a text we can help them become more discerning as readers and less vulnerable to the language of persuasion.

So far, then, we have suggested that the aims of the syllabus could provide a fruitful ground for introducing problems of understanding and interpretation. But we have not reached the central issue which is referred to in a general statement of aims in the Common Core A level pamphlet (and agreed by all the boards):

> To encourage an enjoyment and appreciation of English Literature based on an informed personal response and to extend this appreciation where it has already been acquired.

We welcome the stress on enjoyment and personal response, but the achieving of these aims will always be problematic, given the constraints of the examination.

Many of the issues have been fully discussed in a research report, *Responses to Literature – What is Being Assessed?* by John Dixon and one of the present writers, John Brown (1984). They invited a panel of experienced readers drawn from university professors, school teachers, examiners, HMIs and advisers, representing the whole of the United Kingdom, to look for evidence of response in samples of students' writings from A level examinations and coursework. The report was the first published collection of A level essays which had been scrutinized for evidence of response. The findings of the report can best be drawn from the detailed and scrupulous commentaries of the panel of readers in Part 2, and they are far from encouraging. Overall the evidence of response was not strong, and it was noticeably weaker in the examination essays. There are clear implications for the examining of literature, if only the boards would consider such evidence seriously, especially as it is they who have highlighted students' responses in their aims.

Another reason why all of us who are teachers and examiners need to re-examine our assumptions about reading and response is to be found in the challenge offered by recent critical theories. Many of these have already influenced the design of English courses in higher education and we believe that some are highly relevant to the teaching of A level within the aims expressed by the boards.

In particular, we should want to look carefully at any critical theories which embrace both author and reader. Structuralist critics tend to value the interpretation of texts below that of formulating theories of literary discourse and, at its most abstract, structuralism is abstruse and exclusive. Some critics in this field appear to deny any claim that meaning is individual or personal, and they show scant interest in the social and cultural context of a text. There is, however, a more pragmatic form of structuralism which attempts to comment on the structural coherence of a text. We should like to recommend a recent book, *Literary Theory at Work* (Tallack 1987), which has good chapters on structuralism as applied to two short stories. It must be one of the first books to apply critical theory to texts and to introduce the difficult critical language to students and teachers. It is, however, surprising that among the nine theories discussed in this collection, reader-response is not given a chapter on its own, since that field, along with feminism, seems to us the most relevant to A level as it exists.

We cannot pretend that there exists anything like a clear, unified manifesto by reader-response critics, but they all share a common interest in the active roles of readers in interpreting and responding to texts. This is not the place to trace the history of that movement, but it had its origins in the 1920s and 1930s, in the writings of I.A. Richards, F.R. Leavis, D.W. Harding, and later L. Rosenblatt. There is a continuity of concern from those writers to critics like W. Iser and S. Fish, although they might not welcome being bracketed together. It was Richards (1929) who pioneered the investigation into actual readers' responses, and Leavis (1948) who claimed that reading is 'that process of creation in response to the poet's words', a concept echoed by L. Rosenblatt (1978): 'The literary work of art comes into being through the reader's attention to what the text activates within him'.

Most structuralists avoid the idiosyncrasies of individual readers and look for some permanent, objective properties in the text, whereas reader-response critics see meaning as constructed by the attentive reader in response to textual strategies and expectations generated by the author. Feminism takes this a stage further, and not only defends the reader's right to her own viewpoint but also attempts to examine the validity of the reader's aesthetic judgement (that is, which ideological and political assumptions are being conserved or extended?).

Advancing the reader's status does not mean that any reading of a text is acceptable, and reader-response critics avoid the danger of subjective pluralism by introducing the notion of literary competence. Although the reader is constantly having to make interpretative choices, these will be influenced by her experience of other texts and their generic conventions, as well as her own self-knowledge. Thus critics in this field refer to sophisticated types of adult readers – 'the informed reader' (Fish 1980), 'the ideal reader' (Culler 1975), 'the model reader' (Eco 1979), or 'the implied reader' (Iser 1978). This shared notion of literary competence is flexible, allowing for variations in interpretation rather than presuming that there is a correct or 'normative' elucidation of a text. We can now envisage an advanced reading course with a stated objective of literary competence which is not divorced from students' responsiveness as readers.

The text is not perceived as an independent entity but as something which is created by the reader. So the study of one poem or novel makes the study of the next one easier: the student begins to develop strengths as a reader. What happens in the mind of the reader as she actively constructs meaning and attempts to solve textual problems becomes an important part of the process of interpretation. Thus the study of how students read and how they can be helped to become more discerning readers becomes an integral part of the course.

In a similar way, any study of criticism on an A level course can be largely a study of particular modes of reading which have produced divergent interpretations. It was a new mode of reading by critics like F.R. Leavis, for example, which helped to illuminate the poetry of T.S. Eliot. The study of a book's reception across a few generations of readers will also illuminate the cultural forces which have helped to shape different readings. For example in *A Theory of Communication*, Philip Hobsbaum (1970) examines the changing attitudes to Lawrence's *The Rainbow*.

If we focus the centre of attention on both text and reader instead of on the text alone, both the teacher's and the student's roles will become different. The teacher is no longer the expert exegetist, dispensing authoritative interpretations to students, but an enabler, questioner, supporter, challenger. How these roles might work out in practice is discussed in detail in the main chapters following, but, in general, the teacher will be looking for any evidence of how a student is reading, and finding ways of discussing this with the student. The frequent use of a journal could be one of the most important sources of this evidence. Students can be reassured that there will be room for misunderstandings, for changes of mind, for questions raised by the text, for adventures into speculation, since all of these offer scope for reflective learning and teacher commentary.

Rather than ignoring the simplistic comment or dismissing the purely personal connotation, the teacher can try to probe for the sources of misunderstanding instead of just providing a 'correct' reading. In looking for evidence of response and appreciation the teacher will be able to help the student to distinguish that evidence from rash subjectivity, inattentiveness, or a lapse in memory. This kind of learning is about a variety of meanings and interpretations but within certain limits: students can't just interpret the text as they want to, but they can be sceptical, questioning, irreverent. But if we are to help young readers become more competent, more reflective, more aware, we need to introduce them to a wider range of books than is represented by the A level set books.

A typical A level syllabus will include only a narrow range of genres (drawn from fiction, drama, and poetry), and any good bookshop or library will show students a greater variety of literature from different ethnic and cultural backgrounds, and written in an increasingly expanding repertoire of forms. A contemporary writer such as John Berger finds he has to break the boundaries of genre and experiment with new modes of presentation, as in *Pig Earth*. If an A level course is to have links with contemporary literature (and shouldn't that be an explicit policy?), we need to introduce students to examples of autobiography, biography, oral history, travel writing, documentary, essay, journalism, and so on. Perhaps we can modestly recommend an anthology of writing that one of us compiled with David Jackson, mainly from contemporary writers, *Varieties of Writing* (Jackson and Brown 1984), which includes 'material of quality that respects and confirms a flexible range of ways of speaking, life-styles, perceptions and viewpoints'.

The more widely students read the easier it becomes for them to perceive that all writing depends on codes and conventions, even if only to rebel against, and that some of these conventions were not available to writers at certain times (autobiography was not valued in the eighteenth century). Part of the pleasure of reading comes from developing our abilities to recognize generic signals, allusions, and features. If a reader is prepared to be flexible enough to adjust to the generic markers in the opening paragraphs of a book, she will find it easier to tune into the book's wavelength. Many initial misunderstandings come about because young readers are not familiar with the convention of different kinds of discourse or forms. Even the titles of books often conform to generic conventions (for example, *Nineteen Eighty Four, Fahrenheit 451, Slaughterhouse 5*). Wider reading also helps young readers to understand more clearly why a work of literature seems to have its own frame and coherence, quite separate from the real world it may depict. A student who reads widely will have a closer understanding of a writer's choices about conventions and structures. Moreover, students will also have a greater range of writing to imitate or try their hand at.

To many of us it has always seemed absurd that while candidates taking Art or Music or, more recently, Drama, at A level, are rewarded for creating or performing, the English specialist is denied the role of craftsman or artist. To be fair, JMB includes creative writing as an option, although this has a low priority, but we welcome the elements of creative writing in some of the alternative syllabuses, which form some kind of continuity with writing before the sixth form. There isn't space here to look into the causes of the very narrow range of writing demands at A level, but its origins are to be found in the setting-up of Honours English at London and Oxford Universities in the nineteenth century, when the founders were scholars not writers (for a witty account see Potter 1937). In a course where the predominant (often exclusive) form of writing is the literary essay, the young student has special difficulties in finding her own voice and identity, since she may often be uncertain of what she wants to say. A wider choice of writing, including autobiography, short story, oral history, and so on, may not only help the student to cultivate an individual voice but will also help with her perceptions as a reader. Her journal could include embryonic poems, snatches of overheard dialogue, portraits, descriptive phrases, flashes of insight – the raw materials from which a writer can select, expand, revise, embroider.

In all of this work, the teacher's role will be to encourage the tentative and hesitant voice. The search for a personal voice is always demanding, but even more so for young people when they encounter difficult and profound texts. This is where the role of the journal can be crucial: regular, informal, expressive notes and jottings are reliable modes of writing for a student to attempt to express her insights and perceptions. By its nature, a journal will often be fragmentary, disjointed and uneven, and students will need some kind of reassurance if some of their entries seem undeveloped. Uncertainty and self-doubt can easily tempt the novice to borrow a firmer voice prematurely, from teacher to critic. The first desperate borrowing easily leads to the next, and the next, until the student's own perceptions never surface.

This problem is endemic to all literature courses and needs to be discussed early on. If students want to borrow we should ask them to be strict in their acknowledgements and not try to disguise them. However, if they know that their own half-formed hunches are acceptable, that questions will be welcomed in the place of confident statements, that early explorations are there to be revised and added to, then they may be more hesitant about borrowing from or mimicking critics. We may have to remind them that we're not expecting originality but would like to see a genuine attempt at expressing their thoughts and perceptions. The study of literature for those who are not very confident can so easily become a bogus discipline of imitation, role-play, and masquerade, with a student faking responses and perceptions in order to meet an essay deadline. The search for a personal voice is more challenging but in the end it is more rewarding.

2

PLANNING A COURSE

What turns a syllabus into a course? How can course design be possible in an examination syllabus which includes *Paradise Lost* and *Catch 22*? To say that *Paradise Lost* is the *Catch 22* of its era would not really be sustainable in the teaching or indeed the exam questions! A level examiners have always thought of a syllabus like this as providing a wide range of reading whereas in fact they have often encouraged the narrowing of courses to depth of dubious kind: re-reading, with strong guidance from the teacher, a very small number of texts which together make no course other than one in the single mode of traditional literary criticism: reading for essay writing.

Examiners' reports reveal each year that they recognize that the traditional examination syllabus fails to encourage wholesale fresh, individual writing about the set texts. The recent research by Dixon and Brown (1984) shows in some detail that examination essays, at the end of a two-year course, fail to reveal much evidence of personal engagements with the few texts studied. The double-think of what examiners say they want and the way they actually frame their questions is dealt with elsewhere in this book in more detail. The point to be made here is that wider reading, for example, has clearly failed to be encouraged by the inclusion of a paper of 'unseen' practical criticism. On the contrary, this type of paper has resulted in the narrow practice of technical skills in brief extracts and *ad hoc* poems. In short, as the GCSE National Criteria have recognized, if you want certain qualities to be encouraged in the teaching, these qualities should be the focus of the assessment and the mode of assessment should be framed accordingly. If you want wider reading, for example, you must ask for evidence of it, and coursework writing, whether in the form of accumulated journal comments or single end-of-course reflection, seems the most appropriate method of assessment which the syllabus could demand.

If this argument is followed through it seems to us that failure to produce real personal engagements with texts derives from a failure to turn the syllabus into a course. In our experience performance, even on the worst type of purely technical examination questions, is actually better if students have, for two years, been following a course that, through a variety of reading and writing, has given them certain confidences, skills, and approaches. Commenting on how a writer's techniques create meanings for them as readers and being prepared to be critically responsive to that perceived meaning and its implications, would be one set of confidences, skills, and approaches deliberately encouraged by the course structure and the way it has been put into practice.

So in planning a course the following questions might be helpful. (We shall see how they might be answered in the three course outlines that will follow.)

1 What are the qualities that you want to develop in students as readers on an advanced reading course?
2 What are the qualities that you want to develop in the students as writers on an advanced writing course?
3 How might a range of writing be developed in relation to a variety of reading at different levels of intensive study?
4 What group skills need to be developed for the best type of learning to take place through group talk, listening, improvisations, and presentations?
5 How might the choice of texts now facilitate the qualities identified so far to give unity to the course?
6 How might the timetabling of groups and staff best develop these qualities, perhaps through regular provision for tutorials, seminars, or presentations?
7 What might the course look like as a six-term programme bearing in mind the need for a period of induction at one end and revision at the other?

8 Are there additional resources or events that need to be built into the programme, such as regular theatre visits or the use of hired videos?
9 Can the programme begin to be seen as an arts course that relates to other arts?
10 Is use being made of other areas of the curriculum where relevant?

Different departments will obviously prefer different answers to these questions, one choosing to read a play by Shakespeare other than the set text early in the course, another using the set Shakespeare text but a different novel by Hardy, say, than the one to be studied for examination later in the course. Our own suggestions for induction and final revision are to be found elsewhere in this book. One example of our developing an arts-based approach to a set text, *The Grapes of Wrath*, is available in detail in Gifford and Brown (1983: 146–8). But we would like to provide three examples of different approaches to course planning for three different examination boards as examples of three sets of answers to our planning questions.

First, Peter Daw: Cambridge Alternative Syllabus (9001) – a term's work centred on Ireland 1900–30.

The authors and works chosen for study were Synge (*The Playboy of the Western World*), Joyce (*Dubliners* and *A Portrait of the Artist*), Yeats (a selection of poems from the Macmillan edition edited by N. Jeffares, up to and including *The Tower* volume) and O'Casey (*Juno and the Paycock*). This represents work in all three main areas of prose, poetry and drama, and it should be remembered that this range is important in the first term of an A level course where the skills of close reading and criticism need to be developed, as well as wider reading being promoted.

In the first sessions some attempt was made to explain the political and cultural history of the period which includes the development of Republicanism, the growth of the Gaelic League and work of the Abbey Theatre, the 'Easter Rising' and its aftermath of repression, the Civil war period, and the founding of the Free State. However, this can too easily become a long-winded lecture and most of the detail is best filled in as the texts are being encountered, not beforehand. The study of the history can be brought to life by films or slides, by listening to records of the famous rebel songs, or by looking at biographical and other texts, such as the recently broadcast *Mother of all the Behans*, the early parts of which are most relevant. I have found that students rapidly develop an interest in the period because of the still tragically divided situation in Northern Ireland today, and because the struggle for political identity by colonised peoples is a recurrent theme in the history of our century. The interesting question of the extent to which the ancient language and culture of one people (in this case the Myths and Legends used by Yeats and others, or the language of the Aran Islanders by Synge) can be accommodated into the language and culture of another people, can be explored, and paralleled in many other colonial and ex-colonial situations throughout the world.

The Playboy of the Western World can produce mystification when first encountered, but by the (often comic) attempt to render an Irish accent by the teacher and the less inhibited members of the group it can soon come alive in all its humour and vitality. It has a relatively straightforward plot, with scenes that can be acted and used as a basis for improvisation by the class, yet it raises important issues concerning the attitude of Synge towards the Westerners who are his subject, which are discussed by Raymond Williams in his *Drama from Ibsen to Brecht* (1968). The structure of the play, adhering quite strictly to the unities of time, place and action, can be illuminatingly studied too, providing a vocabulary for discussing more complex plays, including Shakespeare's, later in the course. The greatest focus though, is always the language of the play, and after looking at the skilful presentation of colloquial speech in the play, verging as it so often does on the poetic, I have asked students to produce their own play scripts set in places familiar to themselves (the Youth Club or Sixth Form Common Room) which try to reproduce a colloquial style faithfully and interestingly, and the results have been fascinating and effective.

Dubliners is not a text that has to be studied as a whole, although there is much to be said about its overall structure, which is clearly far more than a random collection of stories. Pieces such as *Araby*, like the early pages of *A Portrait of the Artist*, can engender a powerful response in adolescent readers facing the awkwardness of relationships with the opposite sex, and the almost inevitable desire to kick against some aspects of the environment they are growing up in. Perhaps the story *Eveline* is the most evocative presentation of the ambiguous desire to escape from a fettering background while shrinking from the awfulness of actual decision and action. As sixth formers begin to look at the future and their own place in the world, this story can help to objectify some of their tensions and mixed feelings. *The Little Cloud* also faces some of the same issues, while a story like *The Dead*, surely one of the greatest short stories in the language, deserves careful attention, and although less immediately accessible to adolescents in its themes it is both a moving story and a model of careful prose style that amply repays close textual study. The Joyce of the *Dubliners* collection, and even more of *A Portrait of the Artist* can be used as a stimulus for students' own autobiographical writing which can enter a new stage of reflectiveness and maturity at this age, but it is seldom seen because of the tyranny of the literary critical essay in traditional A level courses. The suggestion that aspects of their own life are described in the third person, as Joyce does with Stephen Dedalus, can often be a key to adding that reflective stance to autobiographical writing.

The poetry of Yeats can be an interesting choice both as an illustration of the development of one poet in terms of technique and to monitor changing reactions to social and political events. I have often started by looking at a very early poem such as *Ephemera* (from *Crossways*) to show the yearning romanticism and unfocused vagueness of Yeats's early style (it is interesting to contrast it with Hardy's *Neutral Tones* to sharpen the critique) before moving on to his mature work. However I have chiefly concentrated on the three poems 'September 1913', 'Easter 1916' and 'Nineteen Hundred and Nineteen'. This has not only a mathematical neatness but brings out the subtly altering political views of the poet. The ardent and relatively uncritical desire to revive a 'Romantic Ireland' that is 'dead and gone', and the sharply challenging third stanza, can be constrasted with the clear ambivalence over the dead rebels in 'Easter 1916'. The subtle use of the image of the stone contrasts with the more straightforward 'wild geese' image of the earlier poem, and the repeated use of 'a terrible beauty' economically states the paradoxical response. The third poem is rather too difficult for many students at this stage, but the vision of horror engendered by the combined repression and civil strife is so powerfully conveyed, and the poet's disillusionment is rendered so forcefully, that some comprehension can be guaranteed. This set of poems can engender widespread discussion of our often ambivalent attitude to 'terrorists, or those who sacrifice all for a cause' (suicide bombers in Beirut, to take but one example), while providing ample illustrations for tackling the vocabulary of poetry criticism. It is however quite different to approach such 'technical terms', or ideas, as 'oxymoron', 'paradox' and 'ambiguity' in full awareness of the pressure of conflicting beliefs that render them an essential feature of an artist's complex response to the world, than to encounter them decontextualised in a dictionary of literary criticism. An essay comparing the three poems can be used to good effect here, bringing out as it should, the essential interaction of style and subject matter.

Juno and the Paycock, dealing as it does with the eruption of violence and its tragic consequences in a domestic setting, needs considerable tact on the part of the teacher because of its obvious closeness in some respects to the current problems in Ulster. However as O'Casey's message is clearly to echo the plea for tolerance and humanity of Mrs. Tancred, later repeated by Juno herself:

> Sacred Heart o' Jesus, take away our hearts o' stone and give us hearts o' flesh! Take away this murdherin' hate, an' give us Thine own eternal love,

it should be possible to avoid any accusation of partisanship or overt political involvement. The fact that the agonies of civil war are tackled in a way which is at one remove from the current situation gives a suitable 'distance' yet must clearly benefit from its closeness to what the students will have seen on their T.V. screens in News and Documentaries. Again, it must be stressed, the play is not selected merely as an example to lead up to a discussion of current affairs, but because it deals in a complex and artistically intriguing way with a range of themes, and is worth reading as a considerable, if flawed, work of literature. If approached last in this term of work students benefit from a knowledge of the historical situation and a comparison with Yeats's poems. As well as the serious,

Term 1: Autumn	Term 2: Spring	Term 3: Summer
INTRODUCTORY TERM AIM AT VARIETY:	**SET BOOKS** *The Grapes of Wrath*	*The Caretaker*
POETRY Start anthology (e.g. Dylan Thomas) and try to give some sense of chronology via tips of Eng. Lit. icebergs.	**COURSEWORK TEXTS** *Love on the Dole, Down and Out in Paris and London, 1984*	*The Birthday Party, Macbeth*
DRAMA e.g. *Under Milk Wood*		
PROSE: FICTION e.g. *Strange Meeting, Washington Square*	**PRACTICAL CRITICISM**	
PROSE: NON-FICTION e.g. *Lark Rise to Candleford*	Use this time to provide variety, widen reading experience and plant ideas. Keep poetry anthology going throughout remaining terms.	
	HAZARDS	
	Sixth Form exams. Introduce idea of long essays.	O Level Lit. exams. Students choose final subjects for long essays. ILEA A Level Summer School – July

tragic intensity to the play there is of course the comedy of Joxer and the 'Captain' which is easily enjoyed, but perhaps open to some of the same criticisms as Synge's plays in its presentation of the Irish working class. The play is a good springboard for a discussion of the mixing of comedy and tragedy which will probably be relevant to the later work on Shakespeare, and the class will usually be divided as to how successfully the two modes are blended in this play, or more generally how far they can be integrated in one play. How much better to begin such work from a felt response to an accessible text than to begin by arid instruction on Aristotle and neo-classical criticism! There is here an obvious opportunity again for creative writing, with students attempting to

Term 4: Autumn	*Term 5: Spring*	*Term 6: Summer*
King Lear	Don Juan (Cantos 1 & 2)	Revision
Gulliver's Travels, Decline and Fall	The 19th century novel – e.g. Great Expectations, Tess of the D'Urbervilles OR I'm the King of the Castle, Lord of the Flies	
Prose: Malory – Donne	Prose of 18th and 19th century (including contemporary criticism).	Exam Practice
Mock exams: Nov/Dec.	Coursework folders to be completed by end of term.	Folders to be moderated – May.

produce either a play script or short story where domestic comedy is used to enhance, by contrast, the effective presentation of a tragedy. Finally the class will need to discuss the presentation of Mary's relationship with Bentham, and the subsequent betrayal, as a symbol for the treatment of the Irish by the English, and assess whether this symbolic function interferes with the realism of the characterisation.

(Daw 1986)

Second, Jane Ogborn describes the Crown Woods School's two-year course for AEB A level, syllabus 7539. In more detail a little more than half a term's work on one text at the end of Term 1 is described.

6 Week's work on *Washington Square*

Lesson content	Students' activity	Aim to encourage
Week 1 (last week before half-term)		
(a) Group pooled expectations of first chapters of any novel.		The idea that ways of reading are transferable to other texts.
(b) Read Ch. 1 aloud. Discussed (a).		
(c) Read Ch. 2.	Given novel to read over next 1½ weeks.	Independent reading.
Week 2		
Compiled agenda for rest of term:	Undertake fact-finding.	Research.
– factual details they need information about;	Where/When/Who/What Events. Chapter chart	Appropriate note-making and record-keeping.
– main aspects of book they wish to attend to.	to keep while re-reading. (Written work 1.)	Questioning of the text.
Week 3		
(a) Feedback from research.		
(b) Read key encounters between Dr Sloper/	Pairs volunteered to take scenes.	Re-reading/revision.
Catherine – dialogue dramatised. (Agreed to		
start with these characters in Week 2 above.)	(Written work 2,3,4.)	
Dr Sloper/Morris: Morris/Catherine.		
Week 4		
Interviews with characters:	Questioning/answering of characters in role.	Discussion of presentation of character.
Dr Sloper; Mrs Penniman, Mrs Almond, Catherine,		
Marion, Morris and minor characters.		
Week 5		
(a) Closer look at final section of novel.	Re-read Chs 34 and 35 in preparation for	Re-reading/revision.
Chs 25 – end.	discussion.	
(b) Group discussion about Morris' motives for		
returning.		
Week 6		
(a) Work on section of Ch. 29 (p. 138) to look at	Isolate in passage words which convey attitudes/	Close attention to language.
way James conveys his characters.	judgements towards people described.	
(b) Work on wall posters illustrating particular		
features of the novel.		
(c) Essays set.	Students chose own essay titles, or modified mine.	Awareness of nature of writing task.
	(Written work 5.)	

(Ogborn 1984)

Third, a Head of English has outlined for us the course he and his department construct around the set texts of the JMB's traditional A level.

A course for a traditional examination syllabus

Term 1

  Introduction: Prose and novel
  Extracts: Jane Austen, *Mansfield Park*
  Blake, *Songs of Innocence and of Experience*
  Introduction: aspects of poetry, e.g. metre, symbol, metaphor
  Introduction: library, resources, etc.

Introduction: Arthur Miller
  Read *Death of a Salesman*

Introduction: Shakespeare
  Read a play (not set text) some sonnets.

Term 2

  Continue Austen. Read *The Crucible*, watch video
  Begin reading *View from a Bridge* and *All My Sons*
  Continue Blake, including paintings/illustrations; look at the
  eighteenth-century social conditions and some literature
  Begin reading *King Lear*
  Essay writing: technique, planning, style, etc.

Term 3

  Read *Great Gatsby*: look at other American literature; aspects of
  American society and American Dream
  King Lear: tragedy (particular reference to other set texts), Aristotle,
  extract from *Poetics*
  Possibly read a Theban play
  Read one or more of Shakespeare's late plays
  Introduction to Hardy's *Return of the Native*

Term 4

  Continue Hardy and *The Tempest*
  Pope, *The Rape of the Lock*: look at verse form, Blank Verse,
  Rhyming Couplet *inter alia*
  Satire: pupils write own examples of some of the forms examined
  Philip Larkin: and other post-war poetry

Term 5

  Another text for paper 2. Recent examples have been *The Changeling*,
  Murder in the Cathedral, Chaucer
  Continue *The Whitsun Weddings:*
  'Approaches to Criticism'

Term 6

  Finishing set texts (if necessary): any revision work, etc. pupils' desire:
  Continue 'Approaches to Criticism': wider, general view of the
  literature read
  Exam technique

In terms 4, 5, and 6 we run an optional course. Occasionally we have been able to allocate four to six lessons a week to this but sometimes it has taken place only at lunchtime. Occasionally three teachers are involved in this course. At the end of it pupils may take the S level if they wish. The course covers aspects of the theory or philosophy of literature, for example:

What is poetry? What is a poem?
What is the relationship between art and craft?
What do we mean by meaning?
How do poets communicate?

Such questions usually stem from quotations by writers on their own work and the work of others. It naturally involves looking at a wide range of literature.

We also look at some literary criticism, examining what they say and to what extent their writings are explication, explanation, description, evaluation, etc., for example, we have looked at extracts from M. Weitz, *Hamlet and the Philosophy of Literary Criticism*. This course naturally varies tremendously depending on teacher interest at the time, the pupil's interests, the texts they are studying, and so on.

Missing is the variation of method, e.g. use of diagrammatic approaches, use of computers for essay technique, and a variation of the cloze procedure to encourage close reading of texts, pupil-led thematic approaches, etc.

We tackle a wide range of literature in the area of Paper 3. It is a wide range, e.g. different versions of the opening verses of 'The Gospel According to St John'. The creative writing of pupils varies as well, teachers using this area at different times during the years.

3

AN INDUCTION PROGRAMME

Some schools are able to provide an induction unit for potential students of A level before the end of the summer term, after the fifth-year exams. Here is a brief example of one part of such a unit which we described in our chapter in *English Studies 11–18: An Arts-Based Approach*:

An induction session for Fifth Formers about to join the Sixth Form was arranged, which aimed to indicate something of the range of activities in Sixth Form English, and to begin to forge a working relationship through an exploration of the central idea in Ted Hughes' *Crow* poem 'Lineage'. A part of the Genesis creation story, followed by a Biblical lineage, was read to the class. Then, in groups of three, students were given an envelope containing the separate lines of the Hughes poem. Each group was asked to arrange the lines into a sequence, to create stanza spaces as necessary, and to glue this sequence on to a sheet of paper. The groups gave a choral reading of their version to the class. Then each member of the group was asked to select one line from their sequence to which to add the word 'because' and complete as a sentence on the sheet. The class then listened to a recording of Hughes reading his poem 'Lineage', were given a copy, and again asked to add 'because' to one line each in order to complete a sentence. Next, groups of six were formed and asked to produce a line-age poem of twelve lines, by the process of each member contributing one line and passing the poem on until it had been round the group twice. Finally individuals were asked to tell, in a poem of their own, the lineage story of an object or creature from its earliest form, perhaps through some metamorphosis, to its present condition.

Later work on *Crow* began with groups preparing readings of the following six poems for a ritualised class performance: 'Lineage', 'Examination at the Womb-door', 'Crow's First Lesson', 'Crow Tyrannosaurus', 'Crow and the Sea', and 'How Water Began to Play'. This selection provides a narrative framework through some of the best poems in the book. Work progressed to consider two questions: 'Of what story might these songs be the fragments?' and 'Write the anthropologist's report on the tribe which tells the story of *Crow*. What are their qualities?' Whilst striking at the heart of what *Crow* is about through creative work on the first question, the second question requires analysis and judgement.

(Gifford and Brown 1983)

However, not all students have the benefit of this kind of continuity. There are many who come new to courses in sixth form, further education, or tertiary colleges, and who will be meeting for the first time as an A level group in a new institution. They will have different qualifications (some with O level literature, some with experience of Plain Texts or coursework) and writing talents; some may have grade A in O level Language but without a formal literary qualification. For students with such diverse experience, an induction programme can help them to reflect on their earlier education and introduce them to new concepts and learning strategies.

As students enter a new phase of their full-time education (the final one for many), there is an opportunity to design a programme which will focus on different kinds of learning and raise questions about the pleasures and problems of literary study. Initially we can offer students working in small groups greater responsibilities than individuals, and the consequential sharing of ideas, resources, and problems may help to increase the commitment of all concerned.

It is not easy to identify staging points in a student's understanding and appreciation of literature because the processes of development and maturation are so complex in young adults, but we can try to share with them our own aims and objectives, and be more explicit when we introduce new activities. In the sections that follow we describe a series of activities that can be used in an induction programme.

Genres and conventions: group presentations

The aim here is to explore some simple concepts about genre and convention by inviting groups of students to prepare a series of poems for reading aloud. We were surprised by the number of students who told us that they had not read any poetry during their fifth year, and were not used to reading aloud. As F.R. Leavis said in a little-known lecture on *Reading Out Poetry* (1979): 'The reader of poetry who doesn't do a great deal of full reading out won't be able to read out in imagination.'

The task needs to be carefully explained: the public reading is to involve all the voices in the group, and the aim is to produce a first reading aloud for others. From our experience, it's useful to suggest to a group that they begin at once with a shared sight-reading of the poem aloud, rather than all reading privately. One student in each group can act as observer / recorder, keeping notes on problems and disagreements. Discussion will inevitably centre on the use of different voices, on rhythm, on stress, on pitch and volume, and these cannot be separated from talk about meaning.

BALLADS AND OTHER NARRATIVE POEMS

Traditional ballads are meant to be read (or sung) aloud, so they make an appropriate starting place, and there are plenty to choose from (e.g. 'Sir Patrick Spens', 'Lord Randal', 'The Twa Corbies', 'Barbara Allen', 'A Lyke-Wake Dirge', and so on). Twentieth-century narratives are sometimes more puzzling, and we have used W.H. Auden's 'O What is that Sound?' and '"O Where are you Going?" said Reader to Rider', 'anyone lived in a pretty new town' by e.e. cummings, and ballads by Charles Causley.

After the shared readings (if each group has been given the same group of poems), the recorders can be invited to swap notes, with the teacher in the chair. It may be useful to have some prepared questions, which the teacher can introduce at relevant points, or give to the groups to take away to discuss, for example:

1 Why did a group share out the lines in that way? Did it help with meaning, rhythm, or stress?
2 Were there any words, images, or phrases which caused problems for the readers?
3 Summarize the story – what is left out? What else is going on in the poem? Are there other components in the poem, apart from the story, which attract attention?
4 Do the modern poems share any other features with the traditional ballad other than metrical form?
5 If there is more than one point of view in the poem, does the narrator (poet?) seem to identify with or sympathize with a particular stance?
6 What would be the problems of transforming the poem into other media, e.g. sequence of drawings, radio play, short story?

The ballad is a fairly easy form to imitate or parody (and there are many good examples, from Thomas Hood and Lewis Carroll to Roger Woddis), and it is a form used still by modern poets (*Crow* – Ted Hughes), so there are ways of following these sessions with both creative work and further readings.

SONNETS

An alternative group activity is to prepare a sequence of sonnets for reading aloud, the poems chosen for their variety of mood and subject. There is a rich choice in the sonnets of Shakespeare, Donne, Milton, and Wordsworth, and later examples could include 'Spring' (Gerard Manley Hopkins), 'Anthem for Doomed Youth' (Wilfred Owen), 'It was upon a July Evening' (Edward Thomas), and 'Harp' (Thomas Hardy). Recent poets who have used the sonnet include Seamus Heaney in a sequence concerning the death of his mother in *The Haw Lantern* (Faber 1987), Sue Lenier in a series of love poems in *Swan Song* (Oleander Press 1982), Wendy Cope in a group of parodies in *Making Cocoa for Kingsley Amis* (Faber 1986) and Tony Harrison, in poems about his father and his Leeds background, *The School of Eloquence* (*Selected Poems*, Penguin 1984).

If students are given copies of a selection of these sonnets, without the authors' names and in a random sequence, can they identify differences in attitude, tone, and language to suggest that the poems were written in different periods of history?

Teachers wanting to carry out some early work on form and metre can invite groups to identify the characteristic features of the sonnet, using all the examples they have been given.

But the main preoccupation, we suggest, should be with the initial grasp of meaning explored through prepared readings aloud. Such group explorations can equip students with useful knowledge of generic and metrical features.

Literature, ideology, and culture

No list of set books is ever neutral. How often do teachers cry, 'Why that book again? Why not try this one for a change?' Examiners are not obliged to justify their choices publicly, and they could argue, in any case, that many books have already been pre-selected by their cultural status: they are 'classics' or 'great books'. But anyone who has attended an Alternative A level consortium meeting when set or coursework books are being selected will know that established consensus is often challenged. Passions are quickly aroused by the mere mention of a title or author.

On one memorable occasion, two opposing factions would not give way, one defending *Persuasion*, and the other, *The Rainbow*. With no sign of a solution, a quiet voice emerged proposing *The Grapes of Wrath*. Without any further discussion, Steinbeck's novel was chosen and the disputing partners seemed equally satisfied.

Had the chairmen invited the proposers of the three novels to support their claims in detail, what arguments and values might have been tossed around? The supporters of Jane Austen might have declared that there was no other woman author on the syllabus. Others might have argued for the accessibility of the social and political background in the two twentieth-century novels. Another faction might have talked about Lawrence's presentation of human relationships – wife/husband, father/ daughter, grandmother/granddaughter, and so on. A few might have wanted to examine how women are presented in the three books, or asked if all the books were equally acclaimed when first published. Someone might have challenged the suitability of these particular novels (from among the writers' collected works) for young adults, or asked how often they have appeared on the list of set books. A supporter of one of them might have referred to the eminent critics who champion their author. How often do we discuss these kinds of issues with students – rarely, if at all? Perhaps we should make them acquainted early on with the kinds of cultural and ideological struggles which help to promote some authors and not others? What do our students know of class, race, and gender subordination? Of censorship (copies of *The Rainbow* were destroyed by the police when it was first published)? Of the recent growth of publishing houses committed to the publication and reprinting of works by women authors (for example Virago and the Women's Press)?

If we want to introduce students to the complex relationship between literature and culture, some early perspectives on the status of the set books is a good place to start. We are not advocating a full-scale introduction to the sociology of literature, but rather some openings and inquiries, based initially on their own rather limited knowledge of how books are promoted and revalued, lose or gain popularity. They will certainly be aware of the reprinting of 'classics' and popular books to coincide with new television or film productions, but they may know little about the power of certain publishers, critics, or journals.

As we said in our introduction, it seems important that students are made aware of the changing reception given to various books or plays, and of the fact that different groups of readers and critics have reconstructed meanings. This may help to dispel notions of a 'correct' interpretation and warn students that their own progressive readings of a book will develop and change over a period of weeks and months.

Once the issues have been discussed they can be referred to at any stage in the course, and groups of students can be asked to undertake some small-scale research and investigations, for example, were the early reviews of this particular novel or play favourable? Did the author receive any help and encouragement from other established writers? How often has the book been reprinted? What range of critical studies of the author are still in print? Has the novel been adapted for the stage, film, or television? Are any of the books on the syllabus best-sellers? In what periods of history were the books originally published (this can be shown on a time-chart)? Students would need access to a good library to answer these questions, or worksheets could be prepared with extracts from letters, autobiographies, memoirs, reviews, and so on. This kind of knowledge is relevant to an advanced reading course, so long as it does not replace the attentive reading and study of the texts.

Short narratives

Students joining an A level course often have widely different reading histories: some may be fast, intuitive readers, keen to tackle a long novel or play, while others may read slowly and unsurely, with less confidence in their grasp of meaning. Given such disparity, it can be useful to include in an induction programme a group of short narratives that are accessible and that can be readily shared by all students.

Teachers always have to rely on what is available locally, and they will also have their own favourites. Ideally we would want to include one or two stories by women, at least one piece of non-fiction, for example Orwell's *A Hanging* or a chapter or section from *Truth, Dare or Promise: Girls Growing Up in the Fifties* (ed. L. Heron, Virago 1985), and examples from popular genres, such as science fiction; for example, 'The Pedestrian' by Ray Bradbury (from *Golden Apples of the Sun*). There are a few very short short stories in Hemingway's *In Our Time* (1929), such as 'Cat in the Rain'.

We might also look for stories which have a range of openings: dialogue ('In the Train' – Frank O'Connor), description ('Cat in the Rain'), exposition ('The Man who Loved Islands' – D.H. Lawrence), action ('An Episode of War' – Stephen Crane), interior monologue ('For Esme – with Love and Squalor' – J.D. Salinger). If these opening paragraphs are photocopied students can be asked in groups to predict what kind of story or narrative follows (see later works on the openings of novels in Chapter 5).

Notes can be made informally, or the teacher can structure this initial work:

1 Is the reader immediately involved, or kept at a distance?
2 Are there any problems in entering into the world of this opening?
3 Are there any unfamiliar references or allusions?
4 Is it clear that the opening belongs either to a fictional or historical narrative as in an extract from an autobiography? What are the signs? Are the distinctions clear or blurred?
5 Does the life depicted seem unusual or typical?
6 Is the reader aware of the author's presence and sympathy?

Questions such as these will help students to become familiar with concepts which can be explored more fully later in the course: the roles of the author and the reader; the framework of the created world; decoding allusions.

Having worked on these prediction exercises, the groups will be ready to read together a complete story, such as the brief 'Cat in the Rain'. This could be read aloud twice by different readers, before exploring certain issues.

POINTS OF VIEW

Are the reader's sympathies with the wife or the husband, or with neither, or with both? Do the reader's sympathies change during the story? Where is the author's sympathy? What is the evidence?

A SENSE OF ENDING

Do the students find the ending satisfactory? Does it close the story or provoke the reader into continuing the story in her own imagination? Students can be invited to draft an alternative ending which suits the development of the story. These endings can be dramatically presented in small groups.

How has the story been changed by these alternative endings? Has a student drawn on particular clues or hints earlier in the story? Then, returning to the original ending, students have the opportunity to reconsider their earlier impressions and comments.

A SUMMARY

Since Hemingway's story is so short, it is not too difficult a task to attempt a summary in about fifty words – a mini-saga! Students can swap summaries and look for features, characters, and details which are left out. Are there important omissions? Do any of the summaries offer interpretations (for example by commenting on the state of the marriage, or by making judgements about characters)? From these notes students will begin to distinguish between the story and the way that story is told. If they were not aware of the author's presence initially, the group activities may have given them a clearer view.

INTERPRETATIONS

Students can be invited to role-play a critic's forum, adopting such roles as:

1 An advocate of feminism.
2 An exponent of sexual symbolism.
3 A sociologist preoccupied with power structures in society.

Teachers may want to choose other viewpoints, perhaps providing examples of analysis from books that the students have read. This is a sophisticated form of role-play, but it is an attempt to introduce a range of viewpoints to show how they may influence the interpretation of a story, and to illustrate briefly how such different interpretations might be supported and justified.

There is an important final task: each individual should have the opportunity to write a short interpretation of the story, after further reflection, which could include any remaining doubts, questions, and uncertainties. Some teachers may want to make this the fourth stage, omitting the role-play exercise.

Most of the work in this induction programme is designed for groups, and that is why there are fairly tight frameworks and sequences. The aim in these opening sessions is to raise a number of key issues, and to encourage students to learn from each other. The teacher is the director, but it is to be hoped that the main learning will occur in the groups.

Depending on the overall course structure, a teacher may want to limit the range of work in these opening sessions and concentrate on one aspect only – poetry, or short stories, or drama. Then in the later stages of the course some initial exploratory group activities can still be designed as a way of introducing new concepts or groups of texts.

4

STUDYING SHAKESPEARE AND TEACHING PLAY-TEXTS

Teaching play-texts

Before we consider the study of Shakespeare we should like to establish an approach to the teaching of play–texts in general.

THE NATURE OF DRAMA

The study of a play is probably the aspect of work which presents fewest problems for most English teachers. Reading the play in class necessarily involves pupil-participation, and there is obviously wide scope for discussion about characterisation, direction, and so on.

Thus Paul Cheetham in a weak chapter on 'Literature for examinations' in *The English Teacher's Handbook* (Blatchford 1986). His introductory course on 'the three main literary genres' in the first term of the sixth form includes 'a brief survey of the development of tragedy and comedy in the theatre' from Sophocles through Aristotle and Shakespeare to Arthur Miller, and from Restoration Comedy through Wilde to Stoppard. In fact, neither literary lectures nor play-reading with 'pupil-participation' seem to us an adequate introduction to the nature of drama study. Against such complacency we would assert that the study of plays is probably the least understood aspect of English teaching at A level, and that writing about drama tends to ignore the live nature of the art form.

At the centre of much misunderstanding about teaching plays for literature examinations is the English teacher's notion of how meanings are produced in the theatre and the relationship between text and performance.

'The theatrical mode of production', writes Terry Eagleton (1978) 'in no sense merely "mediates" the text.' Interpretations made through performance are particular and physically created but are, above all, explorations of the text's potential rather than mediations of inevitable meanings fixed in the text. *How* it's said, *how* it's done in that particular space with that particular audience creates a concrete meaning in a moment that is also, as Peter Brook puts it, 'written on the wind'. It is as potential for such meanings that we should approach the teaching of play-texts and the study of drama, including, of course, writing about performance.

Robert Protherough, in his chapter on 'Working with plays' in *Teaching Literature for Examinations* (1986), takes this approach and provides an excellent checklist of activities which have a basis more in the nature of drama than 'discussions of characterisation, direction and so on'. We would not wish to reproduce these ideas here, but to indicate briefly some implications of our approach for the study of a text frequently set at A level, *Waiting for Godot*.

TEACHING *WAITING FOR GODOT*

In *Teaching Literature for Examination* (Protherough 1986), Bill Greenwell provides a case study of his preparation of students for the study of Pinter. He brilliantly introduces them to forms and concepts central to Pinter's theatre: dramatic metaphor, not only in language but also in set and action; stylistically 'colloquial' speech; a room as territory; surreal logic in a naturalistic context. All these notions are explored through practical activities before the students even know what the set text is.

In preparing students for *Waiting for Godot* improvisations anticipated many of the potential effects of the play-text and established an understanding of Brecht's dictum: 'In the theatre truth is concrete'. Before mentioning the text we improvised in pairs the possibilities in the basic situation of two tramps passing the time. Discoveries were made of things to do to fill the time, silences were explored and the significance of the smallest actions or states of appearance within them. Comedy double-acts were developed on the models of Morecambe and Wise, Little and Large, and Laurel and Hardy. Timings were worked on and routines taken back into the two tramps sketch, which was then worked on for performance. This took improvised exploration into live meaning-making.

The question of suicide cropped up in several improvisations and the opportunity was taken to discover the effect of a conversation on this subject when one of the tramps has his trousers round his ankles (the final image of the play-text). Into one of the performances the teacher introduced a Lucky-figure to whom the two tramps had to respond in front of their audience. In this way the essentials of live meaning-making that underlie Beckett's play-text were realized through practice before we came to the text itself.

At the other end of our work on *Waiting for Godot* in the upper sixth, the group were introduced to some statements from Existentialist philosophers which were juxtaposed with statements by Samuel Beckett. They were then invited to discover if these statements could be related to parts of the play in a way that threw light on the implications of the text.

STUDYING DRAMA AS PERFORMANCE

Drama is rarely engaged with as an art-form in students' writing at A level. Drama actively creates meaning through the participation between actors and audience. Exam questions which refer to dramatic qualities of the play-text do not actually want students to explore interpretations in an actual performance if they have seen one. This is doubly odd because not only are the play-texts written for performance but also some questions would seem to be impossible to answer other than by reference to performance:

> The rich vein of humour in *Much Ado About Nothing* makes a greater dramatic appeal than the more serious scenes of the play. How far is this true for you?
>
> (JMB A level English Literature, Summer 1983)

'Dramatic appeal' is a vague notion if students have not considered the varieties of ways in which drama might be said to make its 'appeal' to an audience in its live exploration of play-text. This question would have required them to have written about performances in some way prior to the examination.

Before looking at how best to offer guidance to such writing, further areas of the study of drama needs to be identified. A number of Alternative A levels allow for students to submit coursework about drama in performance without any reference to the study of a play-text (though there may be, as we shall see, quotation from speech in performance). This is not a challenge to the study of play-texts, of course, but simply an allowance for students to write about a performance of a new play, or simply one for which the text is unavailable for study. The focus of students' writing will still be on meaning and its implications rather than theatre techniques in themselves, such as might be the focus of writing for a Theatre Studies course.

The accusation that this kind of writing is an easy option is based on the very poor model of the instant newspaper review of a performance. In fact, students' work of this kind can be some of the most rigorous and rewarding explorations of meaning undertaken on the course. The following stages in the teaching process involved in this form of drama study give some indication of what can be developed.

1 Preparation for the visit. For the first visit some discussion of key moments of previous memorable experiences in the theatre or some improvisations (such as those in preparation for the study of *Waiting for Godot*) establish the notion of live meaning-making. Students are asked to look out for powerful or subtle 'moments of theatre' in the performance. By this is meant a moment at which the performance suggests meaning to the audience through the uniquely dramatic nature of its medium. Some introduction to the play, the company, the writer, the role of theatre, and the theory behind it may need to be researched and offered to the students.

2 As soon as possible after the performance students make notes in their journals of lines of speech, of their responses to particular moments and scenes they want to discuss with the rest of the group later.

3 These notes are the basis for a class discussion which aims to clarify individual thinking of their 'felt experience'. After this stage more resources may be necessary in the form of, say, the texts of songs, a visit from the director, or a request for an acting text.

4 A first draft of reflective description of the experience, incor-
porating critical thinking about the implications of suggested
meanings, can be made from the notes accumulated so far.
5 Before a final draft is submitted for assessment there may be
a response to it from the teacher, or actor, the director or the
playwright, especially if they are local and can be paid
through the Writers in Schools scheme.

One piece a term of such writing not only provides practice in
improving the quality of the final reflective product, but also
increases the frequency of real insights into the drama itself as
students know increasingly sharply what they are looking for
during a performance. To provide the evidence for these claims
it might be useful to compare two parts of a final essay about
a performance of Frank Wedekind's *Spring Awakening* at the
Sheffield Crucible in 1984.

Tim's essay opens with a confident grasp of the play (which
had not been read):

> The action in *Spring Awakening* takes place in a small close-
> knit community where the adolescent boys and girls grope
> towards knowledge and maturity against the barriers set up
> by their parents and teachers in the name of morality. Despite
> the play being first presented over ninety years ago it holds
> as much relevance today, I feel, as it did then, particularly
> with the current controversy over the morality of surrogate
> motherhood, test-tube babies, embryo experimentation and
> underage sex.
>
> The first theme of the play which we will examine is the
> idea that this moral society, which Wedekind is criticising in
> the play, subjugates natural human instincts. Therefore the
> concept of shame is of central importance to the play and
> something which each of the adolescents suffers from.

Tim moves from summary, to relevance, to theme, to a key
concept with great fluency. Yet so far his writing offers no
evidence that it might have been based on an experience of live
performance. He writes in the discourse of textual study and in
fact he maintains this tone throughout his essay. Ironically he
noticed a reference to a line from *Othello*, which he was also
studying, and it is around this line that Tim discusses the
implications of a vibrant 'moment of theatre':

Perhaps the strongest and most worrying portrayal of shame is the scene in the lavatory where Harry speaks to a religious picture of a naked woman and Wedekind shows the torment in his mind as his natural instincts of desire and lust battle with moral standards which make him ashamed of his human biological instincts.

'It's not your sins you have to die for, but mine. It's for my protection.'

Wedekind is here pointing towards the tragic results which could occur through repressing natural instincts, with Harry 'murdering' (i.e. tearing up) the picture in order to rid himself of his shame.

The play shows the extent of Harry's torment by comparing Harry's situation, of shame and the need to murder the cause of these feelings, to that of Othello's murder of Desdemona to rid himself of his jealousy.

'Have you prayed tonight, Desdemona?'

This line is spoken at the beginning of the scene and suggests Harry's instinctive love and need for the naked woman much as Othello still loved Desdemona as he killed her. Another implication of using the Othello image is to suggest that just as Othello's jealousy was unjustified and created by an evil outsider, so is Harry's shame unjustified and created by the moral society in which he lives.

This seems to us to exemplify a student exploring the implications of language in the context of live drama without the necessity for reference to a play-text. Furthermore, he integrates his other studies of a set book and the discourse of the examination answer with his need to discuss the implications of a powerfully concrete achievement at a specific moment of the drama. Such insight and reflection provide criteria by which this kind of writing can be assessed and moderated, as indeed it is already in several Alternative A level schemes.

Studying Shakespeare

THE PROBLEMS

Shakespeare has always held the dominant position in A level syllabuses, reflecting his special place in degree courses, and yet the study of his plays has not been strongly reflected in most books on the teaching of English (in contrast to the gross over-production of Shakespeare criticism). Little attention seems to be given to how to teach Shakespeare during PGCE courses, because there are more urgent problems. Many young teachers must resort to the practical solution of modelling an approach on a modified version of how they were taught in the sixth form. Indeed many good English teachers who promote active, engaged, personally articulated learning elsewhere in their teaching can find themselves tending to adopt what are really forms of lecturing techniques in their teaching of Shakespeare at A level. The use of a journal, for example, can be completely forgotten when it comes to the Shakespeare set text.

Is that why there are more complaints from our student sample about the teaching of Shakespeare than about any other aspect of the A level course?

We looked at the meaning of every word, but I still didn't understand the play [*King Lear*].

There was a tendency for us to regurgitate facts because we were spoon-fed by the teacher. But he only saw that as sound instruction for the examination.

We never moved out of our desks during eight weeks solid on *As You Like It*. When we finally saw a production I was stunned – it seemed so different, comic and light-hearted.

A lecture-like style of teaching – we merely took notes. Not enough active participation or work.

The teacher expected a kind of half-knowledge for us to be able to discuss enough to show that we knew a lot about it without having formed an opinion. We didn't really need to have read the plays, only an 'exam-passing' booklet.

I bought my own edition and scribbled notes in every margin.

I ended up with a file of notes longer than the play.

We went slowly, line by line. Perhaps this could be improved by studying the play scene by scene, only concentrating on individual lines when the meaning is difficult to grasp.

I'd like to have known how actors prepare a play. Do they take it apart like we did? At least they'd end up with the whole thing. I just concentrated on the main characters for the exam.

Many of the key problems are raised by these students: the understanding of Shakespeare's language and culture; textual annotation; note-taking; styles of teaching; students' lack of participation; the constraints of the examination. There are no easy solutions or fool-proof methods, and we hesitate before suggesting possible ways of coping with these difficulties. To get the most of out of a Shakespeare play requires hard work and responsibility from all those taking part, but the graft can be tempered by creative and productive opportunities. Sometimes the cloak of scholarly awe and respectability surrounding Shakespeare's work can inhibit our experimenting with the plays (there are few such inhibitions in the theatre). There may well be a place on the course, when students begin to feel more confident with the text, for dislocating the play, for cutting scenes or speeches, for treating the play with irreverence. The artistry of the dramatist can often be more clearly perceived when the practical effects of 'cutting' are tried out in workshops, or when scenes are adapted for another medium, such as television or the cinema. But more of that later.

In thinking about possible approaches it is important to try to find out what students have gained from earlier experience of Shakespeare. It seems that many schools now postpone any work on Shakespeare until the fifth year where, apart from the Cambridge Plain Texts O level and some interesting Mode 3 syllabuses, the orthodox examinations offer a poor model. Questions demand knowledge of the plot and character studies, with few opportunities to consider how parts of a play could be staged. There is no incentive in the examination to teach beyond the rudimentary elements and one consequence of such a reductive model for literary study is the spawning of published notes and cribs. Some students report that their schools provide duplicated copies of parts of these cribs, and during the final revision more attention is paid to those than to the texts themselves. Nevertheless, on the positive side, students are becoming familiar with the language of Shakespeare and often see productions in the theatre or on video. Many of the students interviewed said that the main effect of the fifth year study of Shakespeare was to make them look forward to more advanced work.

Editions and other problems

Disappointment followed swiftly for some who found the sheer bulk of textual annotations in some editions very off-putting, notably the 'Arden' (the recent *Hamlet* runs to over 500 pages and is better used as a reference book). The message seemed to be that the play can be understood only after all footnotes and editors' comments have been digested. The very format, with some pages bearing more notes than text, turns the play into a museum piece rather than a script for reading and performing. There are always problems of stockroom inheritance, but one solution is to persuade students to buy their own copy – say the 'New Penguin', 'New Swan', or 'Cambridge', where the text is uncluttered, and strongly urge them not to write in the margins (the beneficial demands of the Cambridge Plain Texts O level set a good precedent). We shall return to this issue in the section on 'Textual annotation' (p. 43).

Another problem we shall consider later is that of the use and abuse of criticism. With library shelves overflowing with books on Shakespeare, only a full-time specialist can hope (or wish?) to keep up with them, and so what can the busy teacher do? How many of us return to critics we found helpful on our degree courses? What advice do we offer students overwhelmed by the profusion of titles and opportunities?

There are problems for the novice in studying a Shakespeare play which more experienced readers can too easily forget. By its nature a play's meaning is revealed slowly during the time it takes to read or view it, but even at a first encounter we find ourselves driven towards some kinds of general statement in an effort to grasp the play as a whole. At the same time we're involved in other kinds of thinking – predicting what might happen, hearing echoes from earlier scenes, being puzzled by the complexities of narrative or language, changing our minds about a character or situation. Some of these thoughts and impressions may stay with us, some may be fleeting, but they may cumulatively prevent us from seeing clearly the play as a whole. If we take a party of students to see a first-rate production, their initial reaction may be one of silence as the power of the re-created play overwhelms them.

How do we encourage students to find ways of thinking more clearly about what they have read or seen, knowing that any general commentary cannot adequately describe the complex emotional and intellectual impact of the forward movement of the play? At what stage in the study of a play do we invite students to attempt more comprehensive statements about the total effect? Are there forms of writing which may help students to grapple with the initial excitements, confusions, and hesitations during the early stages of the course. How conscious are we about stages in the learning process?

We remember when we started teaching in the sixth form how baffled we felt about setting some writing in the early weeks of a reading of a Shakespeare play. We asked for 'notes' on some of the main speeches without really knowing why we were setting the task, and the students' bewilderment was a mirror of our own. It was work for its own sake, with an eye on the final examination, and as unproductive as dictated notes.

In the following pages we want to suggest some approaches to the study of Shakespeare which try to consider learning stages and the appropriate nature of individual and group assignments. Many of the examples are taken from sessions on *Hamlet* with different groups of sixth formers, but other plays are considered as well (for example *The Winter's Tale, As You Like It,* and *Henry IV, Part 1*). At first we were uneasy about offering examples from many different sources, but if we had confined ourselves to one group of students we would have to waste the reader's time with some reports of failures, of badly conceived schemes, or of inadequate follow-up work. What follows is a mixed brew of examples from our own, and colleagues' experiences. We offer it in the spirit of work to be tested and modified.

Re-creating the play

Perhaps because of his pre-eminent status, both in the theatre and in the field of literary studies, Shakespeare seems to attract absolute and uncompromising attitudes. In a recent article in *The Use of English*, Pafford (1985) declares: 'First acquaintance with the text should be hearing it read or spoken aloud as well as can be contrived', echoing comments made over sixty years earlier in a government report on *The Teaching of English in England* (Newbolt Report 1921). There the teacher was exhorted to read the play to the class so that 'they get their first impression from a skilled and understanding reader'.

Although both writers may be referring to younger pupils,

their inflexible stance is not uncommon, and the learners are seen as passive receivers, with the authority of the teacher increased by the authority of text. Surely, with sixth formers, there are ways of giving them more responsibility and initiative, especially with texts which are meant for actors and producers?

We are not dismissing the value of readings, recordings, videos, film and theatre productions, for we see these as playing a crucial part in the interpretation of texts (and would like them to be more publicly recognized in examination questions), but they will all be coloured by the ideologies and preoccupations of the directors and producers. That point is worth making right at the start of the course, so that later any version of the play can be introduced by the teacher with a brief commentary on the interpretation (for example Orson Welles's highly romantic view of the decline of Merry England, personified, as he saw it, in Falstaff, resulted in a sentimental version of *Henry IV* in his magnificent film *Chimes at Midnight*). It seems to us that students need to become increasingly aware of the role of reader/actor/director as mediator of the text; there can never be a neutral interpretation of the play.

As a substitute for listening to a recording, a cursory sight reading of the play, however, is largely a waste of time, because of the language difficulties. As a preliminary to close reading and interpretation it is better to give students time to prepare active renderings of key scenes which offers them greater responsibility for initial interrogation of the text.

The clearer the guidelines we can offer students the better, ensuring that each of them has an active role, as readers or directors, so that no one is merely a spectator. Taking the opening scene of *Hamlet*, we invite students to form groups of three or four to prepare a first reading aloud, urging them to refer to glossaries or editors' notes only if they come across unfamiliar words. The task is to prepare a clear first rendering, so that the commitment to presentation includes the initial grapple with meaning. Problems and questions will arise, and the 'director' should keep notes on these in a form that can be shared later with other groups, perhaps best as questions. Some of the suggestions made earlier for an induction programme (p. 21) will help students to gain confidence for prepared readings.

Group activities in the early part of the course have special value. We remember from our sixth form days being asked to annotate scenes in advance as homework and then being tested next lesson. The work was difficult and unrewarding and there was no sense of working on a script towards some kind of interpretation. The shared group preparation spreads the burden and increases confidence in speaking Shakespeare's language.

A reading aloud will almost certainly raise questions about space, movement, entrances, and exits. Is everyone on stage being addressed by the speaker? Are there moments of reflection, as if the character is talking to himself? How do characters receive unexpected news or information? Such questions inevitably lead to speculation about production and staging, and can be tested out in alternative renderings. It helps if the students know they will be giving their readings in a drama studio or large space, so that relative volume, stress, tone of voice, and simple movements can be rehearsed.

It may help in these early stages if all students do similar work, even if it means three or four different renderings of the scene, because the questions noted by the groups' 'directors' are more easily shared. Readings can be spaced apart during the lesson, so that discussion and interpretation can be readily linked to a new or revised rendering.

At this stage the teacher can decide how far to identify for students the stages of learning implied in the sequence of activities. The more responsibility we offer students the more they need to know about the demands we're making of them. We know how easily we slip into routine teaching strategies where we, as teachers, are more active than our students. One way to encourage more participation from them is not only to delegate tasks so that the students take a more central role, but to share our thoughts about teaching and learning.

Careful planning will be needed, so that groups can work separately on key scenes and speeches, and continuity can be maintained with the use of records and cassettes for less important scenes. There is an opportunity to negotiate with students about the way groups are formed (it may be useful if students who share the same overall timetable work together so that they can meet informally during free periods), and much of their homework can be the practical preparation for reading aloud.

Interpretation

Hopefully the prepared readings will give groups the confidence to discuss each scene in class to more purpose than if they had just undertaken a sight reading. However, even if there has been some kind of responsive engagement with the script, some students may still be struggling with the intricacies of the narrative. One way to check whether students are grasping the details of the story is to ask them to summarize a scene from the point of view of one of the key characters. Story-telling and summary (especially with regard to plays and novels) provides a firm foundation for most readers, especially if it is expressed in their own words (not copied or dictated). The groups preparing readings need to know that one of their jobs is to try to tell the story clearly.

In addition, a group working on a practical presentation of the opening of *Hamlet* will almost certainly be forced into making interpretations that are central to the issues in the play. A consideration of how those opening exchanges are to be said, and from what distances, with some thoughts about movements, is bound to lead to the question of what effect is being made for the audience. A useful next stage is to invite students to make notes in their journal about the implications of the opening of the play. Jottings on the sentries' physical nervousness and unease can be expanded by the later revelation of moral uncertainty in Hamlet's perceptions of the court of Elsinore. The groups of students working on later scenes (for example, when Polonius instructs Reynaldo to spy on Laertes, or where he uses his daughter to lure Hamlet to where Claudius can overhear them) will have the opportunity to test Hamlet's perception against an audience's perception of the court, and the contrast will tell them much about how the play is constructed.

Other issues and problems will emerge when the 'directors' present their group's questions and difficulties. The teacher can help to define these more clearly and distinguish between questions which can be answered directly (most of the textual ones), those which require some historical knowledge and background (for example, Elizabethan attitudes towards the supernatural), and those for which there are no easy answers (aspects of Hamlet's behaviour). Students may be impatient to solve problems but we can try to persuade them to make do with tentative answers or further questions, knowing that later study of the play may provide alternative interpretations.

It isn't easy for students to learn to live with uncertainties but we can plan the course so that there will be opportunities for them to re-examine early impressions and notes. One of the dangers in encouraging students to develop as autonomous readers at this level is that some may find an accumulation of unresolved problems too unsettling and so resort to critics or handbooks for help. Clearly there is a place for criticism on an A level course (which we'll be discussing later), but once students plagiarize early on through lack of nerve the habit is difficult to break. All the more reason, we suggest, to discuss learning strategies with students.

Textual annotation

During early explorations of the script students will need advice about note-making, and this is another opportunity to discuss stages of learning. If our aim is to help readers become more confident in making sense of texts, too many notes will become a distraction, and instead of re-reading the text students can be diverted into glancing at their earlier comments. How can understanding and response develop if the notes of an immature reader are recorded next to the script? As an example, these are the annotations of a girl in the lower sixth on Hamlet's first soliloquy in Act 1, Scene 2:

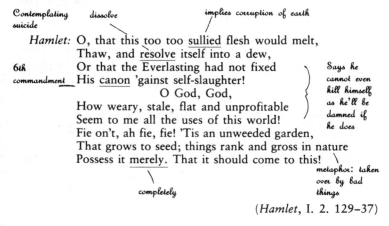

(*Hamlet*, I. 2. 129–37)

Most of the notes suggest a lack of initial confidence in the student in reading for meaning, but will they help at a later re-reading? Isn't it likely that the crude paraphrases will then get in the way? Does the single note on metaphor ('unweeded garden') mean that other metaphors have been understood?

Four words are translated: 'sullied', 'resolve', 'canon', and 'merely' (without reference to textual problems in 'sullied'). Their meanings are likely to be problematic at this simple level only during the first reading. The important thing is to become familiar with their meanings through re-reading and engagement. The opportunity for the latter is provided by the journal where note-making of a personal, puzzling, reflecting type can be made by the student.

When we talked to Carole about her notes she was very forthcoming. She belonged to a group of thirteen students who had made a quick read-through of the play, and her notes were scribbled in later as the teacher discussed the text. There had been no time to prepare the early scenes and she admitted to feeling very unsure about the text and so she had decided to annotate fully. She had not been offered any advice on notetaking, nor had it occurred to her to ask.

Another student, from a different school, had the following notes on the same speech, dictated by her teacher:

> *First soliloquy:* melancholy state of mind. Hamlet is disgusted with the world generally and horrified by his mother's infidelity and the incestuous crime that she and Claudius have committed.
>
> L. 129: 'Sullied' – Three possible meanings:
> 1 Folio 1: 'Solid' – quite a good option – 'melt, thaw'. There are ridiculous connotations – solid means fat, etc. A plump Hamlet? (cf comments in duel scene.)
> 2 Quarto 2: 'Sallied' – meaning fretted, chafed.
> 3 Dover Wilson's emendation – 'sullied', so dirty flesh betrays us. However, why emend if there are already good readings in F. 1 and Q. 2?
> L. 132: He insists the 6th commandment was not God's Law.
>   He cannot enjoy life – 'weary, stale, flat'.
>   He is greatly tormented and so his grammar has gone to pieces.

A good edition of the play will include notes on any crux in the text (L. 129), so why duplicate them? Individual words are given meanings but in both sets of notes there is a generalizing tendency without the close attention that would help the reader to trace the emotional rise and fall of the lines. The comment on lack of grammar could be useful, but wouldn't it be more appropriate to comment on Shakespeare's art rather than Hamlet's aberration, or to devise an exercise that led to this as a discovery articulated in the student's own words! It is always easy to criticize other people's efforts, but what kinds of notes would we advise students to keep which would help at a later reading and during revision?

We would suggest that they try to avoid general statements early on, because they tend to 'fix' Hamlet's character too soon. The group preparations should have coped with the translation of individual words, and we would urge students to trust in their developing powers as readers (the editor's notes are always there to refer to). Some simple questions could be kept in their separate notebook:

1 What do the metaphors convey about the intensity and passion of Hamlet's state of mind which a paraphrase might omit?
2 Which lines or words seem to convey the strongest feelings?
3 What are Hamlet's preoccupations at this stage?

Notes on the text will be of most use if they help the reader to develop an interpretation based on individual and group perceptions, rather than relying on external authority. The use of the journal can facilitate this.

Production exercises and stage conventions

During group preparation of the first scene of *Hamlet*, one of the groups became obsessed with the opening encounters and was keen to work out the possible positions of the soldiers on stage. They asked to work in the drama room with a single spotlight, and they all memorized the opening thirty lines so that they could easily switch parts. Their findings, in the form of three different renderings, were shown to the main body of A level students, and these were some of the issues discussed:

1 Did Shakespeare mean to startle the audience by a sudden start? ('Who's there?')
2 What if the soldiers are so nervous they can only whisper? ('I am sick at heart'.)
3 Surely Bernardo wouldn't appear from an unexpected entrance – the guards would know the routine?
4 Does Bernardo move across stage to take up his watch? ('Holla, Bernardo!')

These questions can be fully explored only if the stage conventions of the time are explored, and this could be the moment to pool ideas from the students' earlier experience of Shakespeare.

There are simple facts to establish about the Elizabethan theatre which we'll simply list here – a theatre open to the sky and therefore without house or stage lights; a stage which projected into the audience, and which had no curtains to rise before the opening lines; the audience were not from a selected section of the community, as they are at Stratford today, but represented all parts of society, from harlot to nobleman; the only scenery was provided by some symbolic structures; all the parts were played by men or boys, as women were not allowed on stage. Most teachers will have their own way of introducing this material, from models of the theatre to slides, and the opening sequence of Olivier's *Henry V.*

At this stage of the work on *Hamlet* not much more needs to be introduced, but there are rich fields to work on if students are to have a strong grasp of the nature of Shakespeare's theatre. Germaine Greer's recent introduction to Shakespeare in the 'Past Masters' series rightly stresses the importance of the audience's active response to a Shakespeare play, and the way the dramatist manipulates that response:

> In order to understand the necessary questions of the play the audience must be drawn into the feelings of the characters, which are displayed for them in monologues, but at the same time they are never allowed to forget their separate existence *qua* spectators. The action of Shakespearian drama is carefully distanced in time and space, topped and tailed with choric commentary. Shakespeare uses all the mechanisms of alienation – self-conscious reference to the theatrical situation, interpolated songs, synopses, dumb-shows, mask figures, comic interludes, anachronisms, topical references, and schematic or symbolic representation of abstract ideas. The audience's own set of values is always relevant; the suspension of disbelief is never total.

(Greer 1986)

Clearly the discussions about staging and production will be illuminated by references both to stage and dramatic conventions so that eventually concepts such as mime and representation can be introduced. However, in these early stages of learning the teacher has to judge just how much information is valuable in helping students to answer their production and textual questions. Some of these may be more easily answered at a later stage when students have a better grasp of the artistic design of the whole play. In the meantime, the teacher can provide brief comments on the way each scene fits into that design.

To return, then, to the production notes on the opening scene of *Hamlet*, we'd like to add a further task. Additional sharing in the interpretation can be promoted if the groups acting as audience during the various renderings of the scene can comment as spectators. One practical way of recording these comments is to pin or stick a photocopy of the scene at one side of a large sheet of paper (the back of unused wallpaper is useful) with space for directors' and audiences' notes, as shown in the diagram. These notes can be added to when students see actual performances of the play and start to compare their initial understanding of the play with other possibilities in the theatre or cinema.

Although we give Shakespeare's text the close attention it demands, this can encourage thinking about parts of the play as if they were static and out of context. Part of the teacher's task is to relate the particular concentration on parts to the dramatic impetus of the whole. This is another reason for avoiding criticism in the early stages, since much of it seems to be based on the play in the head rather than the play to be embodied in performance. The emphasis in much criticism on 'themes' abstracted from the dramatic thrust of the play often seems remote from experiences in the workshop or theatre.

Stage and generic conventions

For a generation used to television and cinema drama there will be some advantages when trying to grasp the conventions of Shakespeare's theatre. The fluid treatment of time and space on the screen is not unlike that in his plays (but helped there by the absence of scenery, curtains, and lighting) and there are modern genres which students understand, for example the thriller, western or science fiction, which offer a useful introduction to generic recognition. The fact that Shakespeare, like many other writers, was an innovator and adapted conventions for his own artistic purposes makes the viewer's (or reader's) growing awareness of generic codes more interesting. As Germain Greer (1986) claims:

Text	Director's questions, etc.	Audience reaction

The Elizabethan audience knew the conventions of revenge tragedy at least as well as we today grasp the complicated rules of spy fiction.

Will a knowledge of the conventions of Revenge Tragedy help students to gain a clearer understanding of the revenge elements in *Hamlet*? We see little value in giving students a potted history of Revenge Tragedy and its conventions before *Hamlet* has been explored initially. The process of abstraction involved tends to establish stereotypes, and inexperienced readers may too readily latch on to these. However, once students have a stronger grasp of the play, Revenge elements, such as 'madness', can be introduced to show how Shakespeare adapts and uses them.

In these early stages the main focus will be on trying to clarify actions and motives, and here some reference to dramatic conventions and Elizabethan beliefs may be useful. For example, Shakespeare's treatment of the Ghost can be explored not only in terms of dramatic conventions, but also in relation to contemporary religious disputes about the supernatural. These are reflected in the different reactions to the appearance of the Ghost by the soldiers, by Horatio and by Hamlet himself. Is it a stage convention that the Ghost speaks only to Hamlet and is not heard by any other character, or is that more convincingly explained by contemporary beliefs about the supernatural?

Similarly, a modern audience's reactions to Hamlet's few references to his legitimate claim to the throne might be very different from that of an Elizabethan audience who would be more mindful of Claudius' usurpation.

To sum up: conventions and beliefs are more easily understood when they relate to specific sections of the play.

Choices about individual work

If we now turn to the second scene in *Hamlet* it is clear that practical decisions have to be made about how thorough the group preparation will be. This scene divides easily into three sections:

1 Claudius and his court.
2 Claudius and Gertrude and Hamlet (including his soliloquy).
3 Hamlet, Horatio, and the soldiers.

Groups could be asked to read the whole scene and then concentrate on one of the sections for more detailed preparation.

Do we ask students to keep to reading the same character parts, or suggest they change from time to time? It could be argued that the role of Hamlet is so important that it should be shared so that all readers have the chance to speak some of his lines and become more familiar with the poetry. On the other hand, if a reader identifies with a particular character and keeps the part throughout the readings, it is possible to understand the play from the point of view of that character and become more involved with that role in the journal.

Thus there may be quite different reactions to a follow-up question about Claudius' treatment of Laertes and Hamlet if the readers are invited to comment in role, that is through the eyes of their character. Hamlet is silent during the early part of the scene, but the reader of Hamlet's part could be asked to provide a running commentary in role as he observes what is going on. The sort of thing we have in mind can be seen in the following example, written by a girl who was exploring the state of mind of a different hero, Lear, before that play begins:

> O to be young again.
> We fear that age and responsibility
> Has so weighed us down,

As to stiffen us and to make us yearn only for
death.
   The pleasures of our youth have fled,
And left us holding so great a weight,
   That we fear it will crush us.
Gone are the days when the affairs of the land
   Were dealt with between hunting and feasting.
Now these cares increasingly worry and weary us
   And we can no longer with such ease, dismiss
them.
We yearn to be carefree and emancipated
   From the chains of responsibility.

If some younger being should relieve us of these
burdens
   Whilst we retained our authority;
Which so fits us like a glove, that to be divorced
of it
   Would be to skin us alive;
We could enjoy our closing years in youthful
freedom,
   Enjoying the cordiality of old friends.

   Our daughters please us.
Their minds are young and enthusiastic
   Eager to assume cares they might one day regret.
All must come to theirs in their time,
   But we see not reason why such able successors
   Should not come to theirs a while sooner.
We do love them dearly, and believe ourself
   To be esteemed high in their affections also.
But we retain the dearest love for our youngest,
   Tender-hearted Cordelia.
She on whom we lavish great affection, might,
   Receive a more generous third than her sister.
We would gladly remain the rest of our days,
   Under her hospitable roof.

Death, we feel, accelerates his pace whilst,
   We are overladen with cares.
In freedom and with renewed vitality,
   We would seek to face death gradually,
In quieter more peaceful places.

                                        (Joanne Merry)

The teacher's comments on this piece were as follows:

> The group had been looking at some of Robert Browning's
> dramatic monologues with a student teacher. When we
> started on *King Lear* I asked them to write as if they were the
> King himself on the way to the court at the opening of the
> play. They did not have to be in verse – and this girl was not
> accustomed to writing poetry.

This kind of exploratory work, but with more psychological
probing, was the foundation for Stanislavski's work in the
theatre. His account of a production of *Othello* offers many
insights into this way of getting inside a character. Joanne's
writing is not of the kind officially recognized by the orthodox
A level but its value in the early stages of a course is self-evident.
It would be relevant as coursework in an Alternative A level.

Identifying with a character or describing part of a scene
through the eyes of a character offers the student the opportunity to get beyond narrative retelling while keeping a sharp
focus on the evidence in the text. The kind of generalizing it
may lead to is related to the particular relationships within the
play at that point, and is not as abstract as many A level
questions; for example 'Consider Lear as a tragic hero'. It is a
more complex task than giving a narrative summary since the
student has to explore states of mind and show the character
looking ahead and reflecting on the past. In Joanne's
accomplished version there are lines which the rest of the group,
or the teacher, might want to question, for example 'We yearn
to be free', and so the words of Shakespeare have to be re-
created again in order to test out that kind of interpretation.
The licence to explore the character has scope only against a
reading of relevant parts of the text.

Later in the course, the students will need help in writing
quite differently, abstracting elements from different parts of
the play and using an expository or argumentative structure. In
these early stages, the focus on role-play narrative is to build on
students' confidence based on their own findings supported by
group interaction.

A bridge between these two kinds of writing can be created
by keeping a diary as one of the main characters, based closely
on his or her speeches only, and excluding, for the present,
comments from other characters. It may help to refer to an
actor's edition of the play where often the lines of the character

are underlined (cf Sher 1985). The diary, unlike the Lear passage, attempts to provide continuity across scenes and acts. The example that follows is selected from a thirteen-page diary of Virgilia, from *Coriolanus*, written by a girl in the lower sixth.

> Civil unrest is growing in this city. The plebians claim to be short of bread. We are all right here though. I'd ask my mother-in-law to give some of our grain to the starving but we don't get on very well together – sometimes I feel we suffer from a mutual feeling of misunderstanding. When Martius came home this evening he was annoyed because of an encounter he had had with various citizens. I left Volumnia to console him in her own way. I expect Martius was rude to the citizens. I did not stay to hear the full story – he is as hard headed as his mother at times. I daresay they will be up half the night discussing wars and politics. . . .
>
> Today Martius left for the wars. Despite the fact there is a chance he will never return I love to watch the departure of the soldiers – there is something almost festive about them. . . .
>
> One of Volumnia's cronies, the Lady Valeria, came today – how I detest that woman! She never comes unless she brings some scandalous piece of gossip. I wanted to leave her and Volumnia to their inevitable war-talk but no, Volumnia insisted I remained. The Lady Valeria putting my short replies down to unhappiness tried to persuade us to go out visiting with her. Needless to say I refused – the thought of an afternoon in her company!

Once again the first-person narrative allows the student to focus on the interpretation of character within the dramatic sequence.

There are a number of ways of following-up this work, to ensure that ideas are shared and tested within a group of students. Simple role-play exercises challenge the student who has spent some time working on one character, for example a press conference, where Horatio is asked to make a public statement about Hamlet's health and state of mind at particular points in the play; Ophelia visits a doctor and tries to give an account of her problems; Hamlet shares his notebook with Horatio; Gertrude is invited by Claudius to offer a fuller account of the closet scene, but she remains mindful of Hamlet's strictures. Providing we advise students not to stray from the evidence in the script, this kind of involvement consolidates earlier work on narrative and character.

However, there is a danger that over-subjective interpretation can lead the student away from the script of the play. The history of Shakespeare criticism shows this nowhere so strongly as in certain famous commentaries on the character of Hamlet, with the hero's being given an extended life beyond the play, for example, Bradley's speculation about Hamlet as a young man at university. The teacher has to be specially vigilant during these sessions and intervene if the participants begin to speculate about events not referred to by Shakespeare. All during the A level course we need to remind students that the artist has selected and structured his material for particular purposes, including its effect on the audience.

In the later section on 'Consolidating work on character' (p. 00) we include a fuller account of an extended role-play session based on *Henry IV, Part 1*.

Using graphics to focus group work

As we have already shown, representational ways of commenting on a script can be easily displayed and amended in the light of further study. The following examples include work on *Hamlet* but refer to other Shakespeare plays as well.

SINCERITY RATINGS

After reading Act I, Scene 3 of *Hamlet*, pairs of students were asked to give a sincerity rating to Polonius, Laertes, and Ophelia on a scale from + 5 (very sincere) to − 5 (phoney). Each pair eventually came and plotted the initials of the characters on a scale on the blackboard, as shown in the diagram.

-5	-4	-3	-2	-1	0	+1	+2	+3	+4	+5
			L	P		O				
			P	L		O				
			L				P	O		
			P	L	O					
			L	P	O					
		P	L							O

| Mean: | | | L | P | | | | O | | |

Here was a basis for class discussion in examining the tone of the language of the text and Shakespeare's patterning of advice-giving in the scene.

INTENSITY GRAPH

On one occasion a first reading of *Hamlet* had reached Act II, Scene 2 and the soliloquy 'O what a rogue and peasant slave am I'. Here we were observing Hamlet's self-analysis and self-disgust. In groups of three, students were asked to consider the fluctuations of the intensity of Hamlet's speech and to judge the extent to which they thought it seemed healthy for his emotional state. So groups were invited to plot on a graph the emotional temperature of the speech in terms of what they felt to be healthy (likely to be resolved in action) or unhealthy (self-indulgence). Each group's final graph was overlayed as shown on the card master-graph.

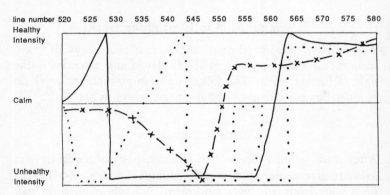

The absence of any agreement was a good starting-point for an exchange of opinion about the amazing processes of change in this soliloquy. At line 535, for example, two groups felt an unhealthy passage had begun, while another thought that he was on the way to a moment of healthy intensity from which Hamlet instantly declined. All groups clearly thought that the ending was strongly positive and likely to lead to action, even to his writing a bit of the play *The Mousetrap*.

SEQUENCING THREE POEMS AND A SOLILOQUY

The 'To be or not to be' soliloquy offered an opportunity for us to pause for reflection on the state of Hamlet's mind. What is his sense of self at this stage? What kind of thinking is at work in this speech? In an indirect attempt to explore these questions groups of three were given the same three poems: 'I Am' by John Clare, 'I Am Vertical' by Sylvia Plath, and 'Wodwo' by Ted Hughes. Groups were asked to consider what these poems and the soliloquy had in common and in what ways they were different. Then they were asked to place the poems in a physical relationship to each other on a sheet of card, indicate a sequence of some kind and select a quotation from each poem. Annotations could be added in a different colour. One group produced theirs in the form of a tree (see p. 56). Attentive work on the language of poets from different periods helped the students to focus their thinking about Hamlet's state of mind.

EMERGING PATTERNS

Pairs of students were given large sheets of paper and felt-tipped pens of two colours, and were asked to represent diagrammatically any patterns they observed to be emerging during *Hamlet*, Act II, Scenes 1 and 2. These would form the basis for group discussions. Below are the results of two pairs' work:

Issues above the surface

1 Polonius employes Reynaldo to spy on Laertes.
2 Hamlet appears in front of Ophelia 'all unbalanced'.
3 Polonius sees Hamlet's madness caused by Ophelia's denial of his love.
4 King and Queen employ Rosencrantz and Guildenstern to find the cause of Hamlet's madness.

Issues below the surface

1 Ophelia not the sole cause of Hamlet's madness.
2 Hamlet is not mad but taking on an 'antic disposition' to find evidence and information.
3 Hamlet sees through Rosencrantz and Guildenstern, doubts their friendship, thinks they have been sent.

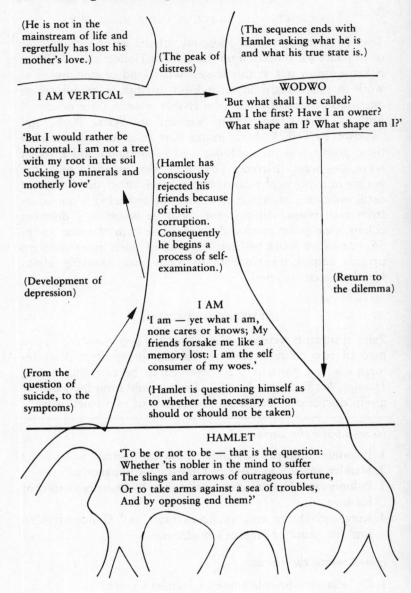

(He is not in the
mainstream of life and
regretfully has lost his
mother's love.)

(The peak of
distress)

(The sequence ends with
Hamlet asking what he is
and what his true state is.)

I AM VERTICAL

WODWO
'But what shall I be called?
Am I the first? Have I an owner?
What shape am I? What shape am I?'

'But I would rather be
horizontal. I am not a tree
with my root in the soil
Sucking up minerals and
motherly love'

(Hamlet has
consciously
rejected his
friends because
of their
corruption.
Consequently
he begins a
process of self-
examination.)

(Development of
depression)

(Return to
the dilemma)

I AM
'I am — yet what I am,
none cares or knows; My
friends forsake me like a
memory lost: I am the self
consumer of my woes.'

(From the
question of
suicide, to the
symptoms)

(Hamlet is questioning himself as
to whether the necessary action
should or should not be taken)

HAMLET
'To be or not to be — that is the question:
Whether 'tis nobler in the mind to suffer
The slings and arrows of outrageous fortune,
Or to take arms against a sea of troubles,
And by opposing end them?'

Spying

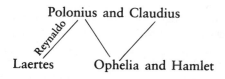

Polonius and Claudius

Reynaldo

Laertes   Ophelia and Hamlet

Themes

1 Pattern of spying
2 Hamlet's madness
3 Rosencrantz and Guildenstern.

A TEACHER'S NOTEBOOK ON *THE WINTER'S TALE*

It is difficult to convey the pattern of teaching techniques that may be used over a period of weeks during the teaching of a Shakespeare play. Imaginative ideas for group work that are too specific may not be appropriate for every lesson's work on the play, especially during a first reading when students will need to spend much of the time in discussion, exploring their own difficulties with the text.

In order to suggest something of this variety of approaches we include in this chapter the first half of a notebook which one of us kept during a lower sixth reading of *The Winter's Tale*. Its function was to record the modes of engagement with each scene and the focus of the discussion so that these could be developed when returning to the play in the following year. An approach should be assumed in which students prepared readings before the lessons and reflected in journals afterwards. Full class discussion followed individual or group work.

Act I, Scene 1: Individually choose one key line to represent the most important information Shakespeare wants to give the audience in this scene.

Scene 2: Write a court reporter's article on the behaviour in this scene, interpreting it for readers, and reporting responses. Quote from what is said.

Act II, Scene 1: Read aloud in pairs, and then as members

of an audience say what has been shown
you here.

Scene 2: In threes list the nature of women's
experience and skills suggested here. What
is your first response? Then consider the
historical context.

Scene 3: Make notes as directors on the stages of
emotional change to be shown in this
scene. Rehearse with three other students,
taking it in turns in groups of four for the
presentation of one of the interpretations
from your group next lesson.

Act III, Scene 1: In pairs decide why you think Shakespeare
chose to put this scene here.

Scene 2: Three students to be asked to take roles of
Laertes, Hermione, and Polixenes. They
are questioned by the class on their speech
and actions in this scene.

Scene 3: This scene is divided into two halves (a)
and (b). Groups 1 and 2 prepare a mime to
express the essence of (a) and (b) respectively. Groups 3 and 4 devise a tableau to
represent the essence of (a) and (b) respectively. Groups 5 and 6 prepare to give us
a talk on the symbolic significance at this
point in the play of (a) and (b) respectively.

Act IV, Scene 1: Prepare a reading that expresses the tone
with which Shakespeare is speaking to the
audience through the figure of Time.

Scene 2: Write Camillo's diary reflections on what
he has learned about the character of
Polixenes today in this conversation,
exploring what he feels about it and his
decisions so far.

Scene 3: Prepare a modern-day improvisation based
upon the slapstick of this scene.

The play as a whole

In describing the approach to a study of a play through
prepared readings and related activities we are aware that
teachers may be anxious about the time this will take, and may

hear grumbles from disgruntled students about losing track of the play as a whole. Certainly when we see a production in the theatre we are often not even aware of the division of acts and scenes as they merge into a larger experience. The problem, in any classroom study is losing a sense of the wholeness, of the continuity of a play.

There are interim solutions, time-consuming but not time-wasting. Once a first reading and discussion of a whole Act has been completed, time can be set aside for a fresh re-reading, without comments, trying to involve as many readers as possible. Or the teacher may prefer to divide the play another way, to help students see more clearly the dramatic structure, and use records or a video at the end of each section.

We have seen in one school the play subdivided, using Hamlet's soliloquies as the main signposts. This certainly helped students to remember their sequence and placing, and the significant events between.

After a prolonged, detailed study of the whole play it is even more important to try to arrange a fresh re-reading of the whole text, even if it means looking for a whole morning or afternoon session when the students are free. During the two years of the course it is useful to plan similar complete readings at specific intervals in order to keep the play alive and help it stay in the memory. With practice students will become fluent readers of difficult texts and familiarity with reading aloud will improve basic understanding. In addition, of course, visits to theatres are essential.

Visiting a performance

A visit to a performance of a play by Shakespeare that is being studied for examination not only highlights the difficulty of distinguishing the differences between text and performance as modes of expression, but also is complicated by the cultural authority attributed to Shakespeare, especially in the institution of the Royal Shakespeare Company. Peter Brook claims:

> The history of the plays shows them constantly being re-interpreted and re-interpreted, and yet remaining untouched and intact.
>
> (Berry 1976)

All 'interpretations' seem possible without disturbing the rich complexity of the texts. The universal overrides the historical, performance is a subservient 'interpretation' of text and Shakespeare's texts are beyond criticism. To a student struggling to make a personal meaning of a text intended for an Elizabethan audience, a visit to an RSC performance can narrow the interpretative possibilities of a play. What is needed is to open up awareness of the process of making personal choices as a student engages with a Shakespeare play.

First, seeing a performance is different in the way meaning is constructed from a reading of the text. This has been argued in an earlier section and a pattern of teaching techniques suggested to help students talk about meanings given by performance. The potentiality for choices of theatrical interpretation needs to be as open and as rigorous for Shakespeare's plays as that of a new unknown writer. Albert Hunt suggests that attitudes to character in performances of Shakespeare's plays are most commonly naturalistic and inhibited from the exploration of theatrical meanings that might be fresh and complex:

> It would never occur to the actor playing the part of the blind Gloucester that, at the moment of his leap from the imaginary cliff, part of the actor's vocabulary might be a somersault and a tumble.
>
> (Hunt 1974)

This suggestion raises choices of dramatic, physical meaning that are clearly different from a reading of a stage direction, and has implications for the values being created at this moment in the play's performance.

Second, we can choose to ignore the historical location of meaning in these Elizabethan plays, as Jan Kott does in *Shakespeare Our Contemporary* (1964), or we can choose between historical interpretations, for example Tillyard's view of Shakespeare as the conservative reactionary reasserting notions of order and authority against the new commercial class of courtiers and the spectre of civil war, or Jonathan Dollimore's historical evidence in *Radical Tragedy* (1982) that Shakespeare's later plays were revolutionary attacks on the status quo of the Elizabethan social structure.

In precise terms, historical facts can lead to historical interpretations from either text or theatrical conventions. That Wittenberg is Hamlet's university, for example, could influence the way Hamlet might be dressed to emphasize his association with radical religious thinking at a progressive university (see New Swan *Hamlet* and Open University Unit *Hamlet*, p. 17). The stage of the Globe Theatre, for our second example, would seem to facilitate an alternation between public scenes on the open platform and private scenes in the inner stage. What would be the effect of reversing the obvious staging at some points in *Hamlet*? What meanings could be suggested about the court in a physical way by playing a court scene in the inner stage?

Third, students visiting the RSC in particular ought to be aware of 'the cultural ethos of "Royal Shakespeare"' that Alan Sinfield analyses in *Political Shakespeare* (Dollimore and Sinfield 1985: 178). The meaning of the spectacular use of expanses of white sheets, for example, might have as much to do with effects related to reviews, other directors, American visitors, or Arts Council subsidies as the context of the performance itself.

To help students encounter some of these issues in preparation for a visit to a performance it might be useful to devise a series of activities based on their choices of 'moments of theatre' introduced earlier. As an example one of us made notes as a member of the group taking part in this exercise prior to a visit to *As You Like It* at the Royal Exchange Theatre, Manchester. Students had been asked to choose three moments in the play whose interpretation in the performance they were particularly interested in observing. Our own attempt is in italics following the instructions to the group.

1 Choose one of the three moments you have an interest in seeing in performance. Write about that moment in any way for about five minutes, exploring whatever thoughts come into your head about it.
   Act II, Scene 4. 'Holla you clown', says the man from the court to the shepherd he's never met before, assuming an arrogance that takes the breath away. We shall probably laugh and feel complicity with the courtier and guilt and wait for a reaction from the shepherd. Corrin knows the score, is a political theorist, has to tell the Fool how rich and workfree he is, entering the economic constraints of Arden.

2 Select one sentence or phrase from what you have written and use it to start again in five minutes' continuous flow.
   'We shall laugh out of embarrassment' i.e. our knowledge of

*the rules of courtesy, codes of showing caring, our expecta-
tion of feelings in the recipient of the arrogance.*

3 Begin your next sentence with the words 'On the other hand
. . .' and continue for five minutes.
*'On the other hand it's not class but human feelings that are
transgressed at this moment.'*

4 Now read over what you have written. Write your notes as
a director, offering suggestions you want to give the actors at
this part of the play.
*'Touchstone: Archly upper class, blindly self-absorbed,
condescending.
Corrin: knowing, judging, should make a slow turn, holding
the moment in his power.'*

5 In groups of three take turns to direct each other, trying out
and changing your notes if necessary. Return to perform this
moment for the whole group to discuss with you.

After the visit to the theatre notes were made in the normal way
on the three selected moments and any others that the performance drew to the attention of each individual. The performance notes on the moment referred to above read:

*Corrin was a serious political informer who nevertheless at
the end of his speech softened to Celia's groans and offered
what he had. Touchstone was flippant, the focus being on
Rosalind's taking charge of the awkward moment quickly.
Later Corrin was seriously straight, not parodying court
'philosophy' when he said 'a cause of the night is a great lack
of the sun?' This is a loss, I think.*

The writing of extended considerations of performances highlight, in the case of Shakespeare's plays, the tendencies towards
generalities and textual conceptions already discussed. The bad
models often provided by public reviews are all the more
common in the case of RSC productions.

Here is an extract from a student's first essay, on a performance of *Hamlet* at Stratford:

The very tone and facial expression the actor used in expressing Hamlet's character was impressive! Every word was an
insult and a moral judgement, a cunning representation of an
intelligent mind struggling between revenge and its own
standards. The only criticism of this portrayal was its
tendency to be too melodramatic. This failing helped lose the

sympathy and understanding of the audience.

(Maria)

Here the generalizations ('impressive' and 'every word') and the distance of the last sentence typify the style of the grand review. Sweeping judgement has prevented the possibility of seeing that melodrama in his soliloquies is a problem for Hamlet too ('O what a rogue and peasant slave am I!'). Yet the spirit of Hamlet's alienation from the court and his historical problem of being called upon to enact a medieval revenge code while wanting to find 'his own standards', as Maria puts it, is sharply described from the 'gesture' of the actor as 'a cunning representation'.

What is needed in practice is writing that focuses on dramatic meaning, along with preparation that helps to establish that focus, if a visit to a performance is of use in answering examination questions that increasingly call for an evaluation of 'dramatic effectiveness'. At the end of the day, after improvisations, directors' notebooks, preparatory discussions, theatre visits, workshops with actors, and journal reflections, the students need an ability to articulate a personal evaluation of dramatic meaning that has both historical and physical theatrical awareness of the potential of the script or text.

Consolidating work on character

We want to give a brief account of a simulation exercise which gave students responsibility for organizing their thoughts about characters, and challenged them in role to prepare careful defences against agreed questions. This simulation was part of the final stages of work on *Henry IV, Part 1*, and every student had an active role.

Four volunteers agreed to take on the roles of Prince Hal, Hotspur, Henry IV, and Falstaff, and they each had two other students, acting as lawyers, to support them. All the students were invited to submit questions they would like to put to these characters if they were to stand trial and defend their actions in the play. The final list of questions was agreed by the group, who then went away to prepare their defence. They had a week to do this, and on the afternoon of the trial a few borrowed costumes added to the excitement. As teacher, one of us acted the part of Lord Chief Justice, but while three students were defending their particular character, the rest could ask supplementary questions. In this way, the simulation was partly prepared and partly impromptu. Only evidence from the text could be used, or references to productions (the group had also read key scenes from *Richard II* and *Henry IV, Part 2*, had seen Orson Welles's film *Chimes at Midnight*, and had enjoyed a production of *Henry V* at Stratford). The list of questions agreed by the group as a whole were as follows:

PRINCE HAL

1 Did you prefer the company of Falstaff to that of your father?
2 What did you admire in Falstaff?
3 What do you think you learnt from him?
4 Don't you think you should have made it clear to Falstaff what would happen eventually?
5 Some accuse you of being consciously treacherous to your friends. What is your answer?
6 In what sense do you feel prepared for kingship?
7 Do you feel guilty about your relationship with your father?

HOTSPUR

1 Why did you join a rebellion against the king, when you were one of those who helped him to the throne?
2 You are accused of selfishness and over-exaggeration – have you any comments?
3 Many find your views on honour outdated. How do you defend your concept of honour?
4 Some people say you lack common sense about political realities. Please comment.
5 Why do you think many actors have preferred to play your part rather than Hal's?

HENRY IV

1 Why are you so concerned about 'popularity'?
2 How have you tried to cope with your troubled conscience about the usurpation of Richard?
3 Why did you fall out with the nobles who helped you to the throne?
4 What are your views on Hotspur?

5 In what ways were you different from your son when you were younger?
6 Why do you think your son, Hal, keeps away from your court?

FALSTAFF

1 Did you ever suspect that your relationship with Hal would one day come to an end?
2 What did you hope to achieve from that friendship?
3 You are accused of callous behaviour towards your soldiers – explain what went on.
4 Many accuse you of cowardice, both during the robbery and on the battlefield. Defend yourself.
5 What kind of a king do you think Hal will be?
6 Why do you think that you appeal to audiences so strongly?
7 How did you feel after the newly crowned King Henry V had spurned you in public?

As can be seen, most of the questions referred to critical moments, conflicts, differences of opinion, but some referred to the deeper issues in the play, such as of kingship, rebellion, and usurpation, looking backwards to *Richard II* and forward to *Henry IV, Part 2* and *Henry V*. The texts of the plays were referred to frequently and students made impressive links between different scenes. Any disputes about interpretation of speeches were fully aired, with the teacher trying to ensure that the trials reached their conclusion. Each 'trial' lasted three-quarters of an hour, so the whole session was a full three hours, with a break mid-way. The challenge in the questions drew a level of commitment and participation from all the students involved.

The use of critics

For teachers and students at any level the sheer profusion of Shakespeare criticism poses problems: for the teacher there is the daunting task of trying to 'keep up' with the ever-expanding repertoire of critical approaches; for the student the hopeless feeling that there is nothing she can say which has not been said many times before. Whatever she puts in her essays will seem like some form of plagiarism. This kind of insecurity can often drive students to take copious notes from critics and try to disguise their provenance by paraphrase. Students will know that one of the main qualities they will be examined in is their 'response to literature, jointly affective and evaluative' (from JMB aims and objectives), and if they find texts difficult to cope with, they will learn a form of role-play and use critics and handbooks rather than struggle to find their own voice.

We've earlier reported some recent research carried out by one of us with John Dixon, *Responses to Literature – What is Being Assessed?* (Dixon and Brown 1984), in which a significant proportion of examination essays at grade B and D, as well as those at O, showed little evidence of involvement or 'possession' of the texts in the view of the panel of readers (who represented university professors, examiners, HMIs, advisers, and teachers). The detailed comments by the panel on individual scripts pointed to three or four key elements:

1 The lack of personal pleasure and involvement, of that 'possession' of the text which makes writing about it worthwhile – and thus, the failure to betray any disturbance, individual reactions, or personal feelings;
2 the substitution, instead, of received ideas, notes, inaccurate annotations, garbled memories, all of them evidence of a mind not on the imaginative work;
3 a distancing from the imaginative experience, so that what is written becomes external, prosaic, tidy, uninspired, stock, mechanical or drilled;
4 the reduction of problems and perplexities within the poetic work, in the effort to categorize, classify and create a neat, well-ordered essay, and cope with the terms of the question perhaps.

The evidence in the report, which is too detailed and complex to summarize faithfully here, suggests that the doubts and misgivings many of us have about the examining of Literature may be well founded, and there are implications for all who teach and assess Literature courses.

But there are other concerns as well, which made us realize how difficult it is to offer advice about the use of critics. We have found ourselves going through a radical reappraisal of our own literary education and of our past and present teaching approaches. The so-called crisis in English studies has centred on a range of new theories – structuralist, deconstructive, ideological, psycho-analytical, and feminist – which challenge not only the curriculum in English courses but also the very structures within academic institutions. On the whole we welcome the pedagogical implications of recent theories because they have helped us to gain new perspectives on our teaching.

However, as we said in the introduction, this debate about the nature of English studies has not reached A level at all. A comparison of recent questions to much earlier ones set in the 1930s in the Higher School Certificate (which preceded A level) reveals just how conservative A level is (see Chapter 7 on questions, pp. 142–57). In many cases there have been minimal changes in the language and structure of examination questions. Does that mean that teachers of A level should ignore the current debate and rely on the more traditional Shakespeare criticism, which, like most A level questions, is concerned with the interpretation of language, characters, plot, themes, and form?

This close analytical school of criticism tended to focus on individual plays and offer detailed comments on the text in an attempt to re-stage the play in the mind. Even when it ignored stage performances, the best of this criticism did elucidate by its concern to find a unity in the structure and symbolism of the play. The focus on interpreting the text in detail challenged the reader to return to the play to test out the new insights, for example F.R. Leavis's (1984) analysis of the 'temple haunting martlet's' speech in *Macbeth*. As teachers many of us will recall moments of clarification which we owe to that generation of critics.

However, recent critical approaches have helped the reader to perceive more clearly the problems of interpretation (textual, generic, and cultural), and become more aware of the diversity of meanings which different kinds of criticism and production bring to the text. Instead of looking for a 'correct' interpretation of the play (is F.R. Leavis's account of *Othello* more satisfying than Bradley's?) the teacher can try to help students understand the hidden values and ideologies in differing reconstructions of the play.

A means of achieving this is to study pairs of critics who offer conflicting interpretations. In particular, where there are contrasting comments on a particular speech or scene, groups of students can be invited to search for the critical stances of the writers. (How is Hamlet's character being constructed? What view of Claudius' court is being offered? Are certain issues or themes being stressed or selected at the expense of others?) We are not wanting to intimidate students with brilliant accounts of the play, but to help them understand more about the codes of critical practice, and encourage them to write their own criticism.

Another approach is for the teacher to extract leading propositions from critics without the illustrative supporting evidence. Groups of students can then be invited to find in the play dramatic encounters or extracts from speeches which support, qualify, or refute the case presented. The teacher can help by directing groups to relevant scenes and then share in the interrogation of the critic's arguments when groups present their evidence.

Giving students an active but subordinate role here will help them to understand that a richly complex text such as *Hamlet* can be viewed from many different perspectives, and that each mental reconstruction may select different evidence or reinterpret the same extracts to support its case. Students are not being asked to discuss one coherent account of the play but to test particular propositions against their understanding of key scenes and speeches. The language of these propositions is generally expository, and students will be helped to see how arguments are formulated by critics.

With regard to *Hamlet*, two contrasting views are to be found in G. Wilson Knight's chapters on *Hamlet* in *The Wheel of Fire* (1949) and H.D.F. Kitto's extensive commentary on the play in *Form and Meaning in Greek Drama* (1959). Kitto writes as an expert on Greek tragedy and uses the moral structure of a religious play to try to explain some of the problem areas in *Hamlet*. Wilson Knight, on the other hand, concentrates on the internal structure and symbolism and produces a decidedly eccentric version of the prince. D.H. Lawrence's essay 'The Theatre' in *Twilight in Italy* (1916) could also be used, because his argument is based on general assertions with little reference to the text.

During the interrogation of the critics' main arguments the teacher may have to help in providing possible reasons for the particular critical stance, for example that a critic is keenly aware of the historical conventions of theatre and drama; that a critic is constructing a Christian interpretation or a Marxist one; that a critic seems to be using the licence of a theatrical producer to distort the play; that a critic is concerned with only a few aspects of the play rather than its organic whole; that a critic is using contemporary symbolism to highlight his or her approach, for example viewing Hamlet as a modern undergraduate; that a critic is using post-Freudian psycho-analysis to make a case about Hamlet's relationship with Gertrude.

It is particularly important to link the analysis of critical stances to students' workshop activities on the play, and to any productions they see during the course (see the section on 'Visiting a performance') so that individual and group responses can be aired and challenged alongside those of the critics.

When an important new production is seen there is the opportunity to collect four or five reviews from newspapers and weekly journals, so that a similar interrogation can be carried out, individually by students or in pairs. This may be a more difficult task than with academic criticism since the reviewer may not have the space to reveal fully his or her attitude to the play as well as to the production. Part of the exercise would be to look for clues and references to any hidden assumptions about the text. The students' own notes on the production might then be redrafted so that their own experience in the theatre can be revised in the light of these subsequent discussions. First impressions are important but there should always be opportunities for further reflection and revision.

In addition, if there is time, it might be useful to look at accounts of past productions, in particular a chapter by Braham Murray called 'On your imaginary forces work' in *Teaching Shakespeare* (Adams 1985), which described his production of *Hamlet* at the Royal Exchange, Manchester, in 1983 with Robert Lindsay, and Jonathan Miller's recent book, *Subsequent Performances* (1986), which has an interesting chapter on his changing attitude to *Hamlet* in three different productions. Other useful books are Styan (1977), Davison (1983), and the *Shakespeare on Stage* series (1984).

One of the most illuminating essays we know which throws light on the changing interpretation of text is by a feminist critic, Elaine Showalter (1985), called 'Representing Ophelia: women, madness and the responsibilities of feminist criticism', from an uneven collection of essays by academics, *Shakespeare and the Question of Theory*. Showalter's essay is a detailed attempt to expose the ideology of representation, and to show how meaning is constructed. By studying the history of the way the part of Ophelia has been represented on the stage from the seventeenth century to the present, and by tracing the iconography of Ophelia in European painting and photography, Elaine Showalter demonstrates that

> the representation of Ophelia changes independently of theories of the meaning of the play or the Prince, for it depends on attitudes towards women and madness.

Her conclusion is that different fashionable interpretations of Ophelia's character ('decorous and pious' in the eighteenth century or as a rebellious heroine in contemporary feminist productions) all miss the essentially complex 'Cubist Ophelia' of the text. The essay is a model of sound research, strong argument, and persuasive conclusion. In particular her analysis of the images of Ophelia in art and the theatre help form a useful basis for a wider cultural investigation. (For example, how is Ophelia represented in the comic strip *Hamlet* and in recent films?)

These are only a few suggestions about how to use critics, but we want to advise that the order and structure of a good academic essay on Shakespeare should not be used as a model for student's writing during the early stages of studying a play. The well-structured critical essay may be the fruit of years of study and reflection, and so the extraction of propositions from critical essays is a way of increasing students' repertoire of ideas about a play and to stimulate further thought, as well as showing them that there is no fixed, stable, comprehensive account of a play. During the A level course they will change their minds and develop new perspectives on characters and situations, and these developments should be an exciting part of their study, so that they are always prepared for new insights and ready to take on alternative approaches. The process of reading and study which the A level student is involved in often works in a tentative and untidy way. Thoughts and feeling may come unpredictably, and it may not be easy for a student to gain the confidence to try to explain where they come from. That's why the journal is so important for recording insights and jottings, not necessarily in any systematic way, but as they occur, and for thoughts to be revised, refuted, or supported at any stage of the course.

Of course, it would be helpful if A level questions took account of the developing nature of the students' understanding and response, rather than posing authoritative statements about the texts for comment. Taking stock of where they have reached in terms of advanced reading and criticism would be of real educational value to students. Instead, all too often the temptation is to role-play (as if the candidate has few doubts and problems) just to impress the examiners or answer the questions.

Revising Shakespeare

A Shakespeare set text tends to heighten the difficulties and dilemmas of revision in general. How should the play be re-read? In what way should accumulated notes and essays be used? How can the teacher keep a balance between supportive structures for weaker students and a development of an individual reading of the text? The ideal answer is to devise a structure that tests and deepens a personal reading of the text. The compromise that is offered here is a structure that develops each student's ability to articulate and justify a personal thesis (or argument) about a major aspect of the play. The assumption is that exam questions will deal with major aspects of the play and that in the process of exploring one in depth the others will inevitably be encountered and considered. The obvious danger in this is the common complaint that the candidate has answered a question that has not been set, but practice in the latter stages of the process can alert students to this danger.

First, previous forms of writing (for example, the journal, directors' notes, essays, etc.) should be re-read by each student looking out for signs of personal insights into the play. These may be found in a small note made after discussion, or a query raised in the journal, or fully argued in an essay. These insights should be listed separately, on index cards or on separate pages of a new exercise book. Quotations should be attached to each, to act either as supportive evidence or an area of reference or a qualification of the point. Then groupings of insights should be made, looking for links between points, seeing if a pattern of a centre of interest or lines of argument emerge. A choice can now be made of the title and approach to a mini-lecture which will be delivered for ten minutes to the rest of the group. In preparation for this the play should be re-read in order to add points to those in the chosen grouping. This is a re-reading of the play with a purpose, that of qualifying more carefully the insights originally made. The structuring of the mini-lecture will need headings and paragraph links possibly with help from the teacher. Other students can make notes on it and discuss it in the spirit of helping one student to test out, sharpen, and qualify an individual thesis on the set text.

In the final stages exam-type questions will be set to the group, at first to practise planning and structure, then to prepare a plan for a timed essay, and finally to practise answering unprepared and unseen questions in the specified time.

The role of the teacher in this process is mainly individual and tutorial. Observations can be made on some common areas that will benefit from brief group discussion, but the temptation to do the lecturing in the belief that this will help weak students should be resisted. An active development and sharpening of a personal possession of the text and an ability to articulate it fluently is what is needed.

For specific comments on A-level-type questions see the section on 'Ways of coping with A level questions'.

5

TEACHING THE NOVEL

Some initial problems are discussed first.

Sheer length of a novel

It is easy for experienced readers to minimize this problem, but many teachers have met students in the sixth form who were still not highly motivated readers. Somehow they had progressed so far with no genuine experience of possessing a whole novel through private reading. Of course, a long-term solution is to adopt an English programme which has the reading of fiction and the creating of stories as central activities at all levels. In some schools, where language-centred syllabuses became the fashion, with extended work on topics and themes, the reading of stories often became a marginal activity. A fiction policy which has at its centre the development of personal reading through regular use of class libraries may be an expensive use of resources if properly maintained, but schools which have adopted this policy have clearly given their students a broad base of experience and expertise to bring to their work on novels in the sixth form. (This is not the place to discuss the ideal curriculum, but in passing we notice the growing pressures on schools to focus on communication skills and to link English activities with Media Studies. Something has to go, and reading fiction could become an easy target.)

What can be done about the sheer length of a book? A novel

can be divided up as a serial, and group tasks allocated for each section. Many of the long Victorian novels were first published in serial form and students will be familiar with the adaptation of books as radio and television serials. Group presentation of key scenes may help less motivated readers to see the value of active re-creation of the text which good reading demonstrably is.

Availability

Do we like to admit to our students that novels the length of *Bleak House* or *The Rainbow* can never be present to readers in their wholeness? It is a confession that subverts all examination systems. What may seem an obvious point is worth spending time on, though it is not often aired. (Two books, however, make effective use of the concept of availability: Hobsbaum 1970 and Kermode 1983.) It is just not possible for readers to relate and remember every episode, nuance, or viewpoint, and over many hours of reading and reflection it is inevitable that our insights and sympathies will shift and develop as details fade in the memory. The more inexperienced a reader is the more likely it is that she will have difficulties trying to grasp the book as a whole. The problem is increased if she is uneasy with the style of the writer (for example, the shifting ironies in Jane Austen, or the symbolic emphasis in D.H. Lawrence) and aware that her own system of values is unstable.

Our students may need reassuring that it is a common problem. No matter how unified a novel seems, the actual process of reading over a period of time will make its impact fragmented and patchy. And each reading of the book will result in a different pattern of fragmentation. As Kermode (1983) concludes, 'the illusion of a single sight reading is no longer possible'. If only examiners and teachers could take that statement seriously, we could revolutionize our ways of learning.

As it is, the traditions of the A level examination show a surprising ignorance of the concept of availability, and students are somehow expected to write on a whole book in 35–40 minutes. The dynamic relationship between writer and reader which constructs the novel, and the cumulative, changing impressions and understanding have to be somehow reduced to a static, detached summary:

What part does the historic and distant past play in *Tess of the D'Urbervilles?*

Discuss the significance of Lawrence's powers of description in *Sons and Lovers.*

If young readers have been enthralled and perplexed by the powerful love stories in these novels, such tasks will surely seem an anti-climax to their study? (For a longer discussion on the constraints of questions see Chapter 7.)

Nevertheless, despite the reductiveness of such demands, there are ways early in a course where we can offer students practical help in coming to terms with a whole novel (see section on 'First reading: summaries, for and against', p. 92).

But we need to remind ourselves of another problem where the young are particularly vulnerable. How many times can we remember getting lost in a book, identifying strongly with characters or becoming so absorbed in a story that we skipped minor details until we reached a denouement? There may be other reasons for the absorption:

> It was a peculiar fact that for the two years of my A level course *Sons and Lovers* became almost more real to me than my own life. Paul Morel, the hero, was fighting his painful battle for emotional freedom from a mother who lived through him. . . . It is hard now to understand the enormous impact that book had on me. . . . Perhaps it was because we read it at a time when we were particularly receptive and vulnerable to powerful works about emotion and sexuality.

Such heady excitement may make it more difficult for a young reader to stand back from the book and perceive where the author's sympathies are. Such a highly motivated student will need very different help from that offered to the reluctant reader.

To sum up: the very length of a book means that the reader cannot make use of it all, and what she selects to discuss will vary with her developing experience as a reader. Somehow the examination system is oblivious to these problems.

We would not choose to discuss with students in the early part of the course the particular demands of the final examination, but we would try to remain aware of the problems of availability, and find ways of trying to reduce the disillusionment many students feel as a result of the constraints of the examination.

A number of students who were interviewed (and who are now reading English in Higher Education) expressed concern about these matters:

> The examination seemed to demand a kind of half-knowledge. As a result 'waffle' could get a good grade. We didn't really need to have read the whole of the novel, only an 'exam-passing' booklet.

> Because *Little Dorrit* was so long, the teacher spoon-fed us with summaries and notes. In the exam I remember conscientiously regurgitating those facts.

> After the exam we felt that our efforts during the past two years had not had their fullest expression in the examination because the questions were so limited.

> Ample time should be allowed for gathering themes, etc. together after the actual familiarity with the novel has been acquired, instead of the frenzied reduction of characters and themes to numbered points . . . one is over-schooled and stale by the time of the exam and merely repeats formulae, being terrified to honestly discuss or question an established view.

It seems there will inevitably be a tension between the experience of reading and that of preparing the same book for the A level examination. Are there ways of using this tension in the learning process? It's a question we'd like readers to chew over as they peruse this chapter.

Reading repertoire: the author and reader

All texts are written in the context of their contemporary history and culture, within certain generic conventions (even if in rebellion against these) and often with an intended readership. The ideal reader would be able to draw on a wide repertoire of reading and cultural knowledge against which a new novel could be explored and evaluated. Many students, however, possess a meagre background of reading and are unfamiliar with the changing fashions of literary conventions and the history of different genres.

Are there ways of helping readers to begin to unravel a text on their first encounter, so that among their first impressions the readers can begin to note generic allusions, the author's stance, and other clues which tell them what kind of world they have to construct with the author? We've already suggested (in Chapter 3) initial approaches during the induction period, using short stories, and so the following suggestions build on those.

Having tried to find stories which students might find easy to relate to, the next exercise introduces problems, including those associated with an author's stance and the range of historical and cultural references. Here are four extracts which illustrate different kinds of writing about industrial England (they were given to students without authors' names, to try to avoid premature judgements:

a) Had a very long and exhausting day (I am now continuing this March 4th) being shown every quarter of Sheffield on foot and by tram. I have now traversed almost the whole city. It seems to me, by daylight, one of the most appalling places I have ever seen. In whichever direction you look you see the same landscape of monstrous chimneys pouring forth smoke which is sometimes black and sometimes a rosy tint said to be due to sulphur. You can smell the sulphur in the air all the while. All buildings are blackened within a year or two of being put up. Halting at one place I counted the factory chimneys I could see and there were 33. But it was very misty as well as smoky – there would have been many more visible on a clear day. I doubt whether there are any architecturally decent buildings in the town. The town is very hilly (said to be built on seven hills, like Rome) and everywhere the streets of mean little houses blackened by smoke run up at sharp angles, paved with cobbles which are purposely set unevenly to give horses etc. a grip. At night the hilliness creates fine effects because you look across from one hillside to the other and see the lamps twinkling like stars. Huge jets of flame shoot periodically out of the roofs of the foundries (many working night shifts at present) and show a splendid rosy colour through the smoke and steam. When you get a glimpse inside you see enormous fiery serpents of red-hot and white-hot (really lemon-coloured) iron being rolled out into rails. In the central slummy part of the town are the small workshops of the 'little bosses', i.e. smaller employers who are making chiefly cutlery. I don't think I ever in my life saw so many broken windows. Some of these workshops have hardly a pane of glass in their windows and you would not believe they were inhabitable if you did not see the employees, mostly girls, at work inside.

b) It was a town of red brick, or of brick that would have been red if the smoke and ashes had allowed it; but as matters stood it was a town of unnatural red and black like the painted face of a savage. It was a town of machinery and tall chimneys, out of which interminable serpents of smoke trailed themselves for ever and ever, and never got uncoiled. It had a black canal in it, and a river that ran purple with ill-smelling dye, and vast piles of buildings full of windows where there was a rattling and a trembling all day long, and where the piston of the steam-engine worked monotonously up and down like the head of an elephant in a state of melancholy madness. It contained several large streets all very like one another, inhabited by people equally like one another, who all went in and out at the same hours, with the same sound upon the pavements, to do the same work, and to whom every day was the same as yesterday and to-morrow; and every year the counterpart of the last and the next.

These attributes of Coketown were in the main inseparable from the work by which it was sustained; against them were to be set off comforts of life which found their way all over the world, and elegancies of life which made, we will not ask how much of the fine lady, who could scarcely bear to hear the place mentioned. The rest of its features were voluntary, and they were these.

You saw nothing in Coketown but what was severely workful. If the members of a religious persuasion built a chapel there – as the members of eighteen religious persuasions had done – they made it a pious warehouse of red brick, with sometimes (but this is only in highly ornamented examples) a bell in a birdcage on the top of it. The solitary exception was the New Church; a stuccoed edifice with a square steeple over the door, terminating in four short pinnacles like florid wooden legs. All the public inscriptions in the town were painted alike, in severe characters of black and white. The jail might have been the infirmary, the infirmary might have been the jail, the town hall might have been either, or both, or anything else, for anything that appeared to the contrary in the grades of their construction.

Fact, fact, fact, everywhere in the material aspect of the town; fact, fact, fact, everywhere in the immaterial. The M'Choakumchild school was all fact, and the school of design was all fact, and the relations between master and man were all fact, and everything was fact between the lying-in hospital and the cemetery, and what you couldn't state in figures, or show to be purchaseable in the cheapest market and saleable in the dearest was not, and never should be, world without end, Amen.

c) Staincross is situated about four miles north of Barnsley, on the highest point of the westerly slope of a deep valley that runs from below Barnsley, northward beyond Wakefield to the textile areas of West Yorkshire. From the high points of Staincross there is a clear southerly view across to the Pennines some fifteen miles away, and northwards as far as the eye can see. Dotted about the landscape, like black mountains thrust out of the earth, are the slag heaps of the Barnsley coalfield; monuments to over a hundred years of coalmining in the area, and to the thousands of mining families who have lived and died on the coal it produced, one generation after the other like an unbroken chain stretching through history. Monuments to unbelievable hardship and deprivation, to a history of struggle against nature, against owners and against governments. Monuments to a way of life evolved in the mining communities over the century. It was to one of these communities, in Staincross, that I was born in 1935.

Staincross of the 1930s was typical in most ways of what is expected of a mining village. Long rows of stone built back-to-back cottages, with the largest concentration of dwellings straggled haphazardly around the North Gawber Colliery and the inevitable stack dominating the whole environment. There was a picture house providing the main centre of family enjoyment, four or five pubs, a church and a variety of chapels, each one ironically built in close proximity to a pub. The whole picture was one of drabness, darkness and greyness. But if the buildings were grey the people who lived in them were certainly not. For, like all mining communities, the beauty, the warmth and the cheerfulness was in the people, not in the architecture.

The outer limits of the village also contained some quite beautiful areas of woodlands and agricultural land. It was here, situated over the brow of the hill out of sight of the ugliness, with an unadulterated view of the open countryide, that the middle class of Staincross had their homes. A different community with different values, different ideals, even a different dialect in the same village. For here people sounded their H's, loved their dogs, went to church twice on Sundays and didn't give a damn about coalminers or the brats they produced.

Let me here explain that the bitterness I feel about the whole system which degraded our forefathers had its positive side. The system produced something very unique and very wonderful in human terms, a humour, a warmth, a comradeship, a special relationship, in fact a community. A relationship that is easier to feel than to write about. This relationship grew up not in spite of but because of the poverty. The close proximity in which families were herded in their back-to-back slums, produced a close identification with each other. In hard times poverty was shared by each and everyone in the community. The very slums in which families existed produced its own kind of humour. Streets and estates in Staincross acquired nicknames which became the means of identification. Silly Row and Monkey Park are two that spring to mind. The names are self explanatory, but the families who occupied these dwellings, far from feeling degraded by the derogatory labels bestowed upon them, were fiercely proud of their small community within the community. When the council pulled down Monkey Park around 1957 and moved the whole community into a spanking new council estate, something was missing, vanished out of their lives. The new estate lacks the warmth and neighbourliness of the old cottages. A factor the planners and architects, conditioned to their own middle class values, could not foresee. Far from wanting the middle class utopia of a detached house with a nice lawn and a privet hedge clearly defining the boundaries of their little kingdom, the miners wanted allotments and pigeon lofts, not activities that isolated them, but things that brought them together. This is not a plea for the retention of slums, but rather that the planners should at least understand and show sympathy for the social values of the community for which they construct. For here lies a real danger, lest the community feeling that was born of a common hardship be eroded and whittled away by bureaucrats and slick advertisers eager to sell us their version of the new society. Consume and possess, buy such a product and make yourself the envy of the street: one of our cars would be sure to turn the neighbours' heads. Self, self, self. These ideas are as alien to the mining community I have grown up in and loved as ice cubes in a hot oven.

d) The car ploughed up hill through the long squalid straggle of Tevershall, the blackened brick dwellings, the black slate roofs glistening their sharp edges, the mud black with coaldust, the pavements wet and black. It was as if dismalness had soaked through and through everything. The utter negation of natural beauty, the utter negation of the gladness of life, the utter absence of the instinct for shapely beauty which every bird and beast has, the utter death of the human intuitive faculty was appalling. The stacks of soap in the grocers' shops, the rhubarb and lemons in the greengrocers! the awful hats in the milliners! all went by ugly, ugly, ugly, followed by the plaster-and-gilt horror of the cinema with its wet picture announcements, 'A Woman's Love!', and the new big Primitive chapel, primitive enough in its stark brick and big panes of greenish and raspberry glass in the windows. The Wesleyan chapel, higher up, was of blackened brick and stood behind iron railings and blackened shrubs. The Congregational chapel, which thought itself superior, was built of rusticated sand-stone and had a steeple, but not a very high one. Just beyond were the new school buildings, expensive pink brick, and gravelled playground inside iron railings, all very imposing, and mixing the suggestion of a chapel and a prison. Standard Five girls were having a singing lesson, just finishing the la-me-do-la exercises and beginning a 'sweet children's song'. Anything more unlike song, spontaneous song, would be impossible to imagine: a strange bawling yell that followed the outlines of a tune. It was not like savages: savages have subtle rhythms. It was not like animals: animals *mean* something when they yell. It was like nothing on earth, and it was called singing. Connie sat and listened with her heart in her boots, as Field was filling petrol. What could possibly become of such a people, a people in whom the living intuitive faculty was dead as nails, and only queer mechanical yells and uncanny willpower remained?

The four extracts are from:

a) George Orwell's diary of *The Road to Wigan Pier* from his *Collected Journalism*, vol. 1 (Penguin 1970)
b) Charles Dickens, *Hard Times* (1854)
c) Frank Pearson, 'A Mining Community' from *Essays from the Yorkshire Coalfield*, ed. J. MacFarlane, (Sheffield University 1979)
d) D.H. Lawrence, *Lady Chatterley's Lover* (Penguin 1960)

We ask students to begin by exploring the relationship between the author and reader, to try to recognize the author's presence and say which passages they find more sympathetic. Since two of the extracts are in the first person, and factually based, the authors' roles are not too difficult to identify.

At this stage it is useful to introduce the concept of foregrounding (linguistic features in a passage which attract attention by deviation), since it covers more uses of language than terms like imagery, rhythm, irony, and so on. We have found that if students are asked to search for particular devices of rhetoric, it distances them too early from the cumulative experience of reading, and often makes their attempt at analysis too systematic and mechanical. If instead, we invite students to notice, as they read, *any* features which are foregrounded, it may help them to become more alert as they read and to notice changes in perspective, tone, and mood. The changes occur during the reading, and are often the result of the artist's deliberate choices and constructions. Foregrounding is especially useful, therefore, because it links the way writers construct their books to the effect on the reader's active participation during reading.

Students readily recognize Orwell's stance in passage (a):

> I am very much aware of the author's presence – he writes in the first person and records his feelings and impressions. Much of the language is highly emotive – 'appalling', 'monstrous', and this shows that he is an outsider, looking in, an alien to the city he describes.

> (Alison)

Some students were puzzled by the foregrounding in the last part of the passage, and one commented on Orwell's 'condescending mention of the fire effects created by lights at night'.

He continued:

> After his list of depressing sights 'by day' the author seems to be drawn to the colours and spectacles of the industrial night. Does this piece of fine writing impress the reader? To me the 'flames' and 'serpents of iron' suggest more unpleasant working conditions, and what was foregrounded made me more detached from the writer.
>
> (Chris)

This perceptive commentary led the group discussing a writer's sense of audience while writing a journal or diary (parts of which may be published later).

Alison's analysis of the extract from *Hard Times* was illuminating:

> This extract is quite different in style – the language is deliberately chosen and used for effect. All the information is generalised. The writer foregrounds for effect, e.g. the 'jungle' images stress the inhuman quality of the town, and the use of repetition reinforces the monotony and machine-like quality of Coketown. At times his use of language is like the highly crafted rhetoric of propaganda.
>
> (Alison)

Other students expressed their responses to the passage, using words like 'hopeless', 'gloom', and 'dreadful prison', but Alison seemed more aware of how she was being influenced by the author and was somewhat alienated by the exaggeration and distortion.

The third passage is not by a professional writer, but was a first attempt by a coalminer to put on paper what he felt about his community. At the time, the students did not have this information, but they readily noticed 'his passionate love for the area in which he was born' and his 'equally passionate, almost desperate appeal for understanding'. They were more willing to trust his words than that of the other writers 'because he admits his feelings and explains them', and there is an absence of 'rhetorical devices'. A useful task would be to ask the students to rewrite the passage in the third person so that they would have a different perspective on the narrator.

The presence of the author in the final passage (d) was felt to be more ambiguous, and students on the whole agreed with Roger's comment:

The mood of the extract is clearly intended to reflect the mood of the central character in it. Only an extremely depressed person would notice in such detail the 'utter negation of natural beauty'.

(Roger)

Alison was more tentative, and admitted to not being sure about the purpose of the passage. By examining what is fore-grounded – 'the highly emotive words' and the repetition to reinforce 'a very negative picture of Tevershall' – she also noticed what she thought was evidence of the author's identific-ation with Connie:

> Some of the details are spoken of with such distaste – 'the awful hats' – as to reflect a troubled and depressed woman. But when the writer includes 'rhubarb and lemons in the greengrocers' he gives himself away. Is there anything ugly in vegetables and fruits, which are surely part of the 'natural beauty' the writer admires? Like passage (b), the writer's main concern is to persuade the reader, even if this means identifying totally with Connie.

(Alison)

To test Alison's perception, students could try rewriting the passage through the eyes of an impartial narrator. During later discussion other extracts from the novel could be looked at, where Lawrence is more detached and offers an interpretative commentary on his characters' thoughts and action (e.g. p. 177 in the Penguin edition).

To sum up: this kind of exercise concentrates on the relation-ship between author and reader, sometimes using the student's alternative narratives as a means of interpreting the passages. A next step would be to look at a variety of narrative postures in miniature.

Narrative postures

So far we have tried to avoid using too much terminology. There are some interesting systems in books such as Moffet (1968) and Booth (1983), and some teachers may feel more secure offering these kinds of frames and structures. However, we would hesitate to introduce too many systems in the early stages, because they can easily become barriers to understanding, rather than props. We prefer to set up a series of workshops which give students the opportunity to look at a range of narratives (in extract), and challenge them to find ways of describing the relationship between author, narrator, and reader. The purpose is to try to make them more alert as readers.

As teachers we think we should often remind our students that novels are constructed, and that the writer has the freedom to choose from many different ways of telling. The choices they make are primarily artistic ones, and our reading can become more enjoyable as we grow more aware of the effects of these choices. If students, lower down the school, have read novels which experimented with different narrative techniques (e.g. R. Cormier, *I am the Cheese*; Alan Garner, *Red Shift*), and have themselves had the chance to try out different forms of story-telling, they will be better prepared. Barbara Hardy's definition of narrative as 'a primary act of mind transferred to art from life' reminds us that we are all potential story-tellers with a repertoire of techniques we already use in our everyday lives. Clearly there are huge differences between the stories we tell to explain why things have gone well or badly, and the sophis-ticated narratives of professional writers, but there are useful parallels – in ways of avoiding reaching a conclusion, in inter-rupting one story with another, in linking events which were not simultaneous, in making excuses, in exaggerating, in mocking ourselves (or others), in omitting vital evidence, and so on. All narrative postures are acts of the mind, and where better to explore these than in the openings of novels.

As with so much other class reading, presenting the passage aloud, as if for radio, may often help a group to identify the author's hidden voice and the tone adopted for the rendering is a good starting-point for discussing the writer's attitude to his readers.

Translating the opening into a radio play or film or television script often clarifies ideas about the role of narrator and isolates the problems of cultural and historical background for the modern reader. Are there references or assumptions in a nine-teenth-century novel which need to be dramatically annotated (for example a flashback which supplies information, using two narrators so that brief questions and answers can be introduced)?

We start with a few first-person narratives:

a) 'Call me Ishmael.' (Herman Melville, *Moby-Dick*)

Is this the gesture of a man who wants you to know him, or an abrupt, rather combative stance? Is there any possible significance in the name? What other clues are offered in the rest of the opening (refer to text)?

b) Through the fence, between the curling flower spaces, I could see them hitting. They were coming toward where the flag was and I went along the fence. Luster was hunting in the grass by the flower tree. They took the flag out, and they were hitting. Then they put the flag back and they went to the table, and he hit and the other hit.

(William Faulkner, *The Sound and the Fury*)

What is being described here? Why that way of telling? Does Faulkner's presentation of Benjy's disjointed impressions create sympathy in the reader? What changes would have to be made if this was translated into a third-person narrative?

There are some openings which take advantage of the reader's familiarity with more traditional narrative, as in J.D. Salinger's *Catcher in the Rye*:

c) If you really want to hear about it, the first thing you'll probably want to know is where I was born, and what my lousy childhood was like, and how my parents were occupied and all before they had me, and all that David Copperfield kind of crap, but I don't feel like going into it. In the first place, that stuff bores me, and in the second place, my parents would have about two haemorrhages apiece if I told anything pretty personal about them. They're quite touchy about anything like that, especially my father. They're *nice* and all – I'm not saying that – but they're also touchy as hell. Besides, I'm not going to tell you my whole goddam autobiography or anything. I'll just tell you about this madman stuff that happened to me around last Christmas before I got pretty run-down and had to come out here and take it easy. I mean that's all I told D.B. about, and he's my *brother* and all. He's in Hollywood. That isn't too far from this crummy place, and he comes over and visits me practically every week-end. He's going to drive me home when I go home next month maybe. He just got a Jaguar. One of those little English jobs that can do around two hundred miles an hour. It cost him damn near four thousand bucks. He's got a lot of dough, now. He didn't *use* to. He used to be a regular writer, when he was home.

In both (b) and (c), we can ask students to try to describe the author's attitude both to the character he has created and to the reader. What does the reader have to bring to the text to share with the author in the creation of his character?

Other first-person narratives we have used are:

Mark Twain, *Huckleberry Finn*
Kurt Vonnegut, *Slaughterhouse 5*
Joseph Conrad, *The Shadowline*
John Braine, *Room at the Top*
David Storey, *Flight into Camden*

We would now add *Waterland* by Graham Swift, and the opening only hints at the author's experiments with different ways of telling:

d)   About the Stars and the Sluice
"And don't forget," my father would say, as if he expected me at any moment to up and leave to seek my fortune in the wide world, "whatever you learn about people, however bad they turn out, each one of them has a heart, and each one of them was once a tiny baby sucking his mother's milk . . ."

Fairy-tale words: fairy-tale advice. But we lived in a fairy-tale place. In a lock-keeper's cottage, by a river, in the middle of the Fens. Far away from the wide world. And my father, who was a superstitious man, liked to do things in such a way as would make them seem magical and occult. So he would always set his eel traps at night. Not because eel traps cannot be set by day, but because the mystery of darkness appealed to him. And one night, in midsummer, in 1937, we went with him, Dick and I, to set traps near Stott's Bridge. It was hot and windless. When the traps had been set we lay back on the riverbank. Dick was fourteen and I was ten. The pumps were tump-tumping, as they do, incessantly, so that you scarcely notice them, all over the Fens, and frogs were croaking in the ditches. Up above, the sky swarmed with stars which seemed to multiply as we looked at them. And as we lay, Dad said: "Do you know

what the stars are? They are the silver dust of God's bless-
ing. They are little broken-off bits of heaven. God cast them
down to fall on us. But when he saw how wicked we were,
he changed his mind and ordered the stars to stop. Which
is why they hang in the sky but seem as though at any time
they might drop . . ."

For my father, as well as being a superstitious man, had
a knack for telling stories. Made-up stories, true stories;
soothing stories, warning stories; stories with a moral or
with no point at all; believable stories and unbelievable
stories; stories which were neither one thing nor the other.
It was a knack which ran in his family. But it was a knack
which my mother had too – and perhaps he really acquired
it from her. Because when I was very small it was my
mother who first told me stories, which, unlike my father,
she got from books as well as out of her head, to make me
sleep at night.

And since my mother's death, which was six months
before we lay by the eel traps under the stars, my father's
yen for the dark, his nocturnal restlessness, had grown more
besetting. As if he were constantly brooding on some story
yet to be told. So I would see him sometimes, inspecting his
vegetable patch by the moonlight, or talking to his roosting
chickens, or pacing up and down by the lock-gates or the
sluice, his movements marked by the wandering ember of
his cigarette.

Like Dickens in *David Copperfield* the writer tries to recapture
the child's vision here and there, but what other perspectives are
offered to the reader? Is the narrator the author? What changes
would have to be made in a third-person re-telling?

Finally, we include four other openings which introduce very
different kinds of narrative. How does the reader become aware
of the author's presence in (e) and (f)? What is foregrounded in
the Dickens' extract, and why?

e) London. Michaelmas Term lately over, and the Lord
Chancellor sitting in Lincoln's Inn Hall. Implacable Novem-
ber weather. As much mud in the streets, as if the waters
had but newly retired from the face of the earth, and it
would not be wonderful to meet a Megalosaurus, forty feet
long or so, waddling like an elephantine lizard up Holborn
Hill. Smoke lowering down from chimney-pots, making a

soft black drizzle, with flakes of soot in it as big as full-grown snow-flakes – gone into mourning, one might imagine, for the death of the sun. Dogs, undistinguishable in mire. Horses, scarcely better; splashed to their very blinkers. Foot passengers, jostling one another's umbrellas, in a general infection of ill-temper, and losing their foot-holds at street-corners, where tens of thousands of other foot passengers have been slipping and sliding since the day broke (if this day ever broke), adding new deposits to the crust upon crust of mud, sticking at those points tenaciously to the pavement, and accumulating at compound interest.

Fog everywhere. Fog up the river, where it flows among green aits and meadows; fog down the river, where it rolls defiled among the tiers of shipping, and the waterside pollu-tions of a great (and dirty) city. Fog on the Essex marshes, fog on the Kentish heights. Fog creeping into the cabooses of collier-brigs, fog lying out on the yards, and hovering in the rigging of great ships; fog drooping on the gunwales of barges and small boats. Fog in the eyes and throats of ancient Greenwich pensioners, wheezing by the firesides of their wards; fog in the stem and bowl of the afternoon pipe of the wrathful skipper, down in his close cabin; fog cruelly pinching the toes and fingers of his shivering little 'prentice boy on deck. Chance people on the bridges peeping over the parapets into a nether sky of fog, with fog all around them, as if they were up in a balloon, and hanging in the misty clouds.

Gas looming through the fog in divers places in the streets, much as the sun may, from the spongy fields, be seen to loom by husbandman and ploughboy. Most of the shops lighted two hours before their time – as the gas seems to know, for it has a haggard and unwilling look.

The raw afternoon is rawest, and the dense fog is densest, and the muddy streets are muddiest, near that leaden-headed old obstruction, appropriate ornament for the threshold of a leaden-headed old corporation: Temple Bar.

(Charles Dickens, *Bleak House*)

f) It was late in the evening when K. arrived. The village was deep in snow. The Castle hill was hidden, veiled in mist and darkness, nor was there even a glimmer of light to show that a castle was there. On the wooden bridge leading from the main road to the village K. stood for a long time gazing into the illusory emptiness above him.

Then he went on to find quarters for the night. The inn was still awake, and although the landlord could not provide a room, and was upset by such a late and unexpected arrival, he was willing to let K. sleep on a bag of straw in the parlour. K. accepted the offer. Some peasants were still sitting over their beer, but he did not want to talk, and after himself fetching the bag of straw from the attic, lay down beside the stove. It was a warm corner, the peasants were quiet, and letting his weary eyes stray over them he soon fell asleep.

But very shortly he was awakened. A young man dressed like a townsman, with the face of an actor, his eyes narrow and his eyebrows strongly marked, was standing beside him along with the landlord. The peasants were still in the room, and a few had turned their chairs round so as to see and hear better. The young man apologised very courteously for having awakened K., introducing himself as the son of the Castellan, and then said: "This village belongs to the Castle, and whoever lives here or passes the night here does so in a manner of speaking in the Castle itself. Nobody may do that without the Count's permission."

(Franz Kafka, *The Castle*)

The next opening is from another classic, familiar to experienced readers:

g) It is a truth universally acknowledged, that a single man in possession of a good fortune, must be in want of a wife.

However little known the feelings or views of such a man may be on his first entering a neighbourhood, this truth is so well fixed in the minds of the surrounding families, that he is considered as the rightful property of some one or other of their daughters.

"My dear Mr. Bennet," said his lady to him one day, "have you heard that Netherfield Park is let at last?"

Mr. Bennet replied that he had not.

"But it is," returned she; "for Mrs. Long has just been here, and she told me all about it."

Mr. Bennet made no answer.

"Do not you want to know who has taken it?" cried his wife impatiently.

"*You* want to tell me, and I have no objection to hearing it."

This was invitation enough.

(Jane Austen, *Pride and Prejudice*)

How does a reader respond to that first sentence? Does she hesitate or nod in agreement? Do the next few sentences make her more aware of the author's presence? What tone of voice would convey the author's relationship with the reader?

The final opening, from *Mrs Dalloway* by Virginia Woolf, creates a highly distinctive world. Is the reader aware of the author's presence? If students tried to summarize what goes on here, what would be missing? What is being asked of the reader here?

h) Mrs. Dalloway said she would buy the flowers herself.

For Lucy had her work cut out for her. The doors would be taken off their hinges; Rumplemayer's men were coming. And then, thought Clarissa Dalloway, what a morning – fresh as if issued to children on a beach.

What a lark! What a plunge! For so it had always seemed to her when, with a little squeak of the hinges, which she could hear now, she had burst open the French windows and plunged at Bourton into the open air. How fresh, how calm, stiller than this of course, the air was in the early morning; like the flap of a wave; the kiss of a wave; chill and sharp and yet (for a girl of eighteen as she then was) solemn, feeling as she did, standing there at the open window, that something awful was about to happen; looking at the flowers, at the trees with the smoke winding off them and the rooks rising, falling; standing and looking until Peter Walsh said, "Musing among the vegetables?" – was that it? – "I prefer men to cauliflowers" – was that it? He must have said it at breakfast one morning when she had gone out on to the terrace – Peter Walsh. He would be back from India one of these days, June or July, she forgot which, for his letters were awfully dull; it was his sayings one remembered; his eyes, his pocket-knife, his smile, his grumpiness and, when millions of things had utterly vanished – how strange it was! – a few sayings like this about cabbages.

She stiffened a little on the kerb, waiting for Durtnall's van to pass. A charming woman, Scrope Purvis thought her (knowing her as one does know people who live next door to one in Westminster); a touch of the bird about her, of the jay, blue-green, light, vivacious, though she was over fifty, and grown very white since her illness. There she perched, never seeing him, waiting to cross, very upright.

(Virginia Woolf, *Mrs Dalloway*)

There are clearly other ways of exploring the author's and narrator's presence and attitude, and extracts can be found which illustrate something of the variety of indicators, from detached commentary to elusive hints and suggestions. This focus on particular features of a novel is only a way of trying to raise students' awareness in preparation for a first reading of a novel. Some teachers may think it is too early to introduce work of this kind, and it is always difficult to decide both whether specific tasks are suitable at a particular stage of the course and whether a series of assignments has a useful educational purpose. Is the student being too firmly directed in one direction? How do we help young readers to grow?

There is a great deal of critical discussion about the part the reader plays in the production of textual meaning, with some, like W. Iser (1978), arguing that the reader is a co-creator of the novel. In doing so, the reader is discovering what is already present in the language and structure, and so the book isn't merely a prey to free subjective interpretations. Iser is referring to the experienced reader, capable of recognizing deeper structures and allusions. What is attractive about Iser's phenomenological approach is that he accepts the importance of each individual reader's interpretation. The difficulty for the teacher who, like us, welcomes Iser's position, is to find practical ways of promoting growth which motivates the young reader and does not overload her with too many concepts and techniques. We are not offering a complete programme, only some suggestions for teachers to try out and build on.

First reading: summaries, for and against

One of the main problems for students studying a long, complex novel is to find a way of grasping the structure and story in shorthand terms. During the first reading the twists and turns of the narrative surprise the reader, but most summaries of novels ignore these aspects of the narrative. Is a simple chapter-by-chapter summary of much use at this stage?

Some teachers suggest that after a rapid first reading a summary is a good way of clearing up any misunderstandings. Certainly with a complex novel like *Bleak House*, where multiple plots interrelate, a simplified diagram or chart will be useful. Is it of the same use for a novel like *The Rainbow* where the story, or stories, may not be the reader's main attention? If we want our students to develop as readers is it worth their time concentrating on that one element of the novel? We need to consider what a reader actually does during reading, and see if there are ways of recording some of these activities.

Does the reader readily enter the various episodes and scenes or are there cultural or language barriers? How much sympathy for characters is demanded or elicited? How often does the reader revise her impressions and attitudes and alter her judgements, and how far is the author in collusion? Are there pages which stay in the mind and others which are easily forgotten? Where does the reader need help from other readers or students? Are there questions the reader would like to put to the author?

There are no doubt other reading activities we've left out, but our purpose is to begin to uncover a few of the complex mental initiatives we use in reading and which, on an advanced reading course, we can discuss with our students. It's not a straightforward topic, because we need information from the students about how they perform as readers, so that different habits and strategies can be discussed. One of the most practical ways of studying the reading process is to examine students' reading logs or journals.

Reading journals: *The Rainbow*

A simple stage-by-stage commentary during a first reading is useful for a number of reasons. First, it helps the reader to define some of her difficulties by the sheer effort of putting them into words. Then a narrative form of notes allows for first impressions, random thoughts, flashes of insight, as well as simple story-telling, if the latter makes the reader feel more secure.

The main argument for a journal is that, like the notes after different readings of a poem, it tells us about the learning process, and later revisions and impressions can be added at any stage. In contrast, the simple summary is fixed and unalterable.

The journal is the record of each student's active participation in the construction of meaning over a period of time.

If students have never tried keeping a journal before, some guidelines and examples will be useful. There are good examples of first impression jottings by younger students in a number of books, for example Jackson (1983: ch. 8) and Fry (1981). Many professional writers' journals and letters contain vivid evidence of first reactions to a book, often colloquial and wittily irreverent. That lively and informal model of how adults reflect on books is often forgotten because of the formality of much academic criticism. It helps, too, if the teacher keeps her own reading log and from time to time is willing to share extracts with students.

There isn't space here to quote from adult journals and letters, but we recommend the following:

The Diaries of Virginia Woolf, vols 1–5 (Penguin 1979)
Collected Letters of D.H. Lawrence, vols 1–3 (Cambridge University Press 1979)
Journals of Katharine Mansfield, ed. J. Middleton Murray (Constable 1927)
Collected Essays, Journalism and Letters of George Orwell, vols 1–4 (Penguin 1970).

What follows is an extract from a student in the lower sixth who was keeping a journal for the first time. Jane had studied *Far From the Madding Crowd* in the fifth year and read *Sons and Lovers* during the summer. The notes were made during an initial reading of *The Rainbow*.

> Lawrence writes about the men and women separately – not as individuals. Contrast Hardy. Women seek 'knowledge' – 'not money nor power nor position', but men who have that knowledge belong to middle class e.g. priest. L. refers to 'common women' of village – is that L? or are Brangwen women snobbish?
>
> Ref. to *Odyssey* and *Ulysses* – how important is this? Vivid description of farm cut off by canal and railway – 'on the safe side of civilisation', 'remote and original'. L. seems opposed to industrial revolution.

Family tree:

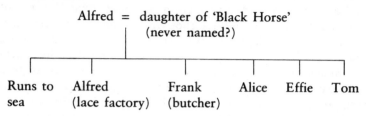

Alfred = daughter of 'Black Horse'
       (never named?)

| Runs to | Alfred | Frank | Alice | Effie | Tom |
| sea | (lace factory) | (butcher) | | | |

Tom very moved by poems but hates books.
Tom's childhood seems sketchy – compare details in *Sons and Lovers*. Father's death seems casual?
Tom seduced by prostitute and disillusioned 'nothingness'.
In home women were like 'angel', 'conscience keeper'.
Para. sums up Tom's feelings about women (some echoes from Paul in *Sons and Lovers*).
Whitsun 'jaunt' – first scene in detail with dialogue, which helps bring it to life. Too much summary before, L. seems in a hurry?

The girl and foreigner both excited Tom – 'they had set fire to the homestead of his nature'. Tom asks himself questions about his life and the 'new influence'. Wants to marry but starts drinking and still dreams of 'Foreign parts'. Seems to be wasting his life?
Strange meeting with woman in black – 'That's her' – like a Hardy scene. 'He moved in the world that was beyond reality.'

Does she remind him of the other girl? Love at first sight? Long dialogue with Tilly, as Tom tries to find out more.
Tom's life changed – 'A swift change had taken place on the earth for him.' L. says – 'It was coming, he knew, his fate. . . . He made no move: it would come, what would come.' Difficult to grasp – why is Tom so sure? Why doesn't he make a move? Too many things in this first chapter.

(Jane)

In their journals, none of the students in the group seemed much interested in the opening paragraphs of the novel, although there was more discussion after these were read aloud. Jane's reference to Hardy was picked up and the opening of *The Mayor of Casterbridge* was read aloud by the teacher. He also referred to a letter by Lawrence about an early draft of the novel – then called *The Wedding Ring* (*Collected Letters*).

All of the group had notes on the women's desire for knowledge, but they had difficulty in grasping what this meant. Having completed the book (not without much difficulty!), the students were able to return to their earlier notes with a better understanding. The search for other kinds of fulfilment, embodied in the lives of particular characters across three generations, fleshed out the rather abstract notions in the first chapter (see the section on 'Further study and reading', p. 99).

We would like to refer in passing to some suggestions for approaches to *The Rainbow* made by teachers in South Yorkshire, Cleveland, and Avon. The teachers were attempting to design activities that might help students to analyse what Lawrence is presenting on those early pages. The sequence of suggestions is random and teachers were invited to try out one or two:

1 Use of landscape paintings to give a sense of isolated communities with anonymous figures in a landscape, perhaps on the edge of a village e.g. Samuel Palmer, Van Gogh, Millais, early photographs. Help from art department and students doing art. How would they re-create the opening?
2 Read poetry on similar themes: R.S. Thomas, Crabbe. Compare openings of other novels, e.g. *Return of the Native*, *Far From the Madding Crowd*. What particular world is D.H. Lawrence creating?
3 Read some social history or memoirs of farm workers – G. Ewart Evans, George Bourne, R. Jefferies, J. Burnett – to give the relevant social history, and then attempt to describe why Chapter 1 isn't social history. How far does Lawrence create a world which is readily accessible to students in the 1980s?
4 Prepare a shooting script of the opening, as a way of understanding Lawrence's perspective on the roles of men and women. Suggest close-ups of scenes of some of the farm activities, e.g. riding horses, feeding geese, killing rabbits, etc. Does it help to see the changing focus of the passage?
5 Use of drama to help to understand the different roles of men and women on the farm. How to show the men's close relationship with nature? How to show the women's desire to look beyond the ritual of farm life, e.g. the church tower, the squire's house, etc.

Brief reports from teachers who had tried variations on (3) and (4) made it clear that there were good accessible social histories which fully documented the roles of men and women, showing how much work depended on women's labour, for example R. Samuel, *Village Life and Labour* (Routledge & Kegan Paul 1975). Farm workers' memoirs include R. Jefferies, *Hodge and his Masters* and *The Toilers of the Field* (both Eyre & Spottiswoode 1949), G. Bourne, *Memoirs of a Surrey Labourer* (Duckworth 1907); J. Burnett, *Useful Toil* (Penguin 1977); and G. Ewart Evans, *Ask the Fellows who Cut the Hay*, *The Farm and the Village*, and *The Days that We Have Seen* (Faber 1956, 1969, and 1975).

To return to Jane's notes, there are other details we should like to comment on. The family tree was an attempt by a number of students to understand the early history of the family. The group were genuinely puzzled by the sketchiness of Tom's childhood, although one girl said that Lawrence used dialogue for the important episodes (cf. Jane's note on the Whitsun 'jaunt'). That particular scene was dramatized, and the group discussed Tom's feelings about women, picking up the reference to Paul in *Sons and Lovers* in Jane's notes.

Her comment – 'Seems to be wasting his life' – took the group back to the text to see if they could find evidence to support it. A number of other students had thought, like Jane, that the meeting with Lydia was like a Hardy scene and they referred to the episode in *Far From the Madding Crowd* when Boldwood, unseen, watches Bathsheba riding bareback. The group found Boldwood's feelings easy to grasp, compared to Tom's, and wanted more from Lawrence at that point in the narrative. An interesting exercise for later might be to try to add further comments, in the role of the author revising the text after consultation with an editor.

We've spent some time discussing students' logs to suggest that collectively the students' experience of reading was a rich source of learning, and it made it easier for the teacher to see where help was needed. It seems to us that on an A level course space should be found for the expression of doubts, questions, changes of mind, and uncertainties because these are crucial stages in genuine personal learning. Coursework elements in an A level would recognize some of these stages, and mitigate the effect of a final examination which seems to demand mature formulations on difficult books. There is a genuine educational conflict here between conditions that promote genuine self-knowledge and those that make for success in examinations.

Stages in the novel

It is easy to divide *The Rainbow* into three narrative structures, so that students can look at the development of each section across chapters:

Chapters 1–3:   Tom and Lydia
Chapters 4–7:   Anna and Will
Chapters 8–16:   Ursula

In their journals students have the opportunity to respond to the struggles in the relationships, to trace their sympathies, and to note the author's judgements.

The same group of students were irritated by Lawrence's treatment of Will, contrasting the vividly presented quarrels and fights between Anna and Will to the loaded authorial judgements against Will. The group became very impatient with Lawrence's repetitive style, and compared the references to 'black will' to some of Hardy's comments on characters.

A similar antagonism was felt towards Lawrence's treatment of Ursula's teacher, Winifred Inger. The group read aloud sections from the chapter 'Shame' and were not convinced that she was a fully created character. One of the students referred back to the early part of Chapter 1 where some characters are just sketched in. These long, agitated discussions about the relationship between the author and reader were a valuable exploration of a key issue in this novel.

In the Ursula chapters students found a less detached authorial presence which led many of them to identify with Ursula, and it was significant that comments in their journals became more personal, even referring to episodes in their own lives. This allowed the teacher to move on to other activities, which we sketch out briefly.

Creative explorations

Where students become very involved with a character, it may be useful to allow them to step back by describing that character through the eyes of another character at a crucial point in the novel, and get them to look more closely at the author's comments and viewpoint. These new perspectives may help the reader to revise their initial personal response and become more critically aware of the author's presence. Like the exercise on the opening paragraphs of novels, inviting students to translate a short episode into a different narrative code (that is third person to first person) also focuses attention on the author as narrator and commentator. Adapting a scene for a radio play likewise concentrates on how a writer's sympathies and antipathies are to be revealed in the presentation. These kinds of exercises make creative demands on the students and they also help to establish some detachment from a particular character.

If A level was conceived as a more balanced reading and writing course, there could be opportunities for students to try out a programme of many different forms of writing. One of the best discussions of how this could be organized can be found in *Active Voice* by James Moffett (1981). Because of the lack of time on an A level course, it has never been possible to establish varieties of writing as a major element in exploring a novel or play.

Further study and reading

During the first reading of the novel, the student's journal acts as a record of her first impressions. Later readings will offer a different view, mainly because curiosity about events and characters can give way to speculation about patterns in the novel, about links between different parts, about motifs and symbols.

These later impressions are very important to record, because they will begin to make the whole novel more available as the student stands back from the narrative. There is still much to discuss and note down: the reader will be revising earlier impressions of the way characters are presented, and it should be possible to begin to distinguish between her own preferences and the author's; she will be having second thoughts on which are the most important scenes or episodes, and perhaps know more clearly where she needs help. This gives the teacher the opportunity to take stock of the group's problems with the novel and find ways of dealing with them.

The group we've referred to located most of their troubles in the earlier parts of the book:

1 They were generally puzzled about Tom's search for fulfilment and by the attitude towards Lydia, but enjoyed the scenes between Tom and his stepdaughter, Anna.

2 The conflict over religion between Anna and Will alienated many in the group, mainly because they could not make the cultural connection.
3 Most were irritated by Lawrence's treatment of Will, and of his inadequacies.
4 They recognized a basic problem of interpretation: that in many ways Lawrence's vivid, sensuous descriptions were not purely realistic but referred to deeper levels of meaning.
5 They were aware of recurring symbols and images but found them difficult to grasp.
6 They felt most positive about Ursula's spiritual longings, her attitude towards her parents (for example, her mother's fecundity), her idealism, her desire to be independent, but were less sure about aspects of her relationship with Skrebensky.

This sketchy diagnosis was revealing, because the teacher realized that it would be better to start with the last section of the book, where the students felt most confident, and help the group to relate back to the earlier chapters. Thus at the stage where the most detailed discussions were taking place the teacher was not, as is so often the case, treating the novel chronologically. By trying to help the group consolidate their grasp of the Ursula chapters (or some of them) he could then invite them to redefine and become more specific about their uncertainties in the earlier chapters.

In particular, when the ending of the novel was being discussed, he asked the group if there were earlier signs that the book would end in that way. Earlier allusions were recalled, and by assigning sections of the book to pairs of students, all references to arches, rainbows, doorways, wayfarers, and journeying were collated. A few of the group were aware of the biblical significance of the rainbow but the teacher did not want to offer his own interpretation of the pattern of symbolism in the novel. Instead, he asked the pairs of students to extract the key references and try to comment on differences in presentation in the three sections of the novel.

It was a crucial stage in the learning process. The students were aware that they were trying to cope with symbols which were suggestive and not always explicit. 'Pisgah mount' had to be annotated by the teacher, and the 'pillars of cloud and fire'. Tentative and fumbling suggestions were followed by more confident realizations that there were clear differences in

Lawrence's descriptions of common symbols (arches, doorways) with each generation.

There isn't space here to follow this through, but the students' notes and charts were their first attempt to interpret, in fairly simple ways, what are, in effect, highly complex parts of the novel. The teacher was deliberately keeping a low profile and trying to allow the group to be actively involved in appropriating difficult pages to their stage of understanding.

Follow-up work involved going back to the reading journals. The discussions on symbolism had made the students more secure about the author's attitudes towards the main characters, and the teacher thought it would be useful for students to try to plot their own developing and changing perspectives towards characters and the writer. This was done in note form, and the first impressions now became more clearly a stage in the learning process, as they were being revised during subsequent readings and discussions. Now many of the students found reasons for their earlier misunderstandings, and for identifying more easily with one character than another at first reading. Space was left in the notes so that later revisions could be added, thus reducing any tendency towards a fixed or final response. The teacher had to reassure the students, time and time again, that altering one's views was not a sign of weakness, provided they were able to reflect on the possible reasons for change, and find relevant supporting evidence in the text.

Occasionally questions appear on the A level examination papers inviting the student to comment on her changing attitude to the set book during the course. If A level was really about the development of a student's literary education, such questions would become more central.

It will be clear that there are still huge areas of the book to explore (the 'moon' symbolism presented many difficulties for the students), but we have tried to sketch out some of the stages in a course which concentrate on the students' growth as readers.

Intentionality

Never trust the artist, trust the tale.

(D.H. Lawrence)

Students are prompt at asking questions about the writer's

intentions, especially when they are trying to get a clearer grasp of his presence in the narrative. In later readings of the novel students become aware that the writer can be present in more elusive ways, for example in a few fugitive words unnoticed during the first reading, or in symbolism and imagery, for example Anna and Will characterized as birds – hawk, plover, eagle. The whole theoretical dispute about intention is a troubled area, and without overloading students with difficult concepts, there are a few issues worth discussing with students in the later stage of study.

We can use a number of sources in a discussion of a writer's intention, and an obvious starting-point is to research the comments of the writer during the creative process and his retrospective reflections after publication. Lawrence's letters are a rich resource, from the one in June 1914 (*Letters of D.H. Lawrence*, vol. 2, no 732 (Cambridge University Press 1981), where he explains his new method of presenting characters, to a brief reference in April 1915 to the novel's 'organic form' (*Letters of D.H. Lawrence*, vol. 2, no 906). This kind of research can be carried out by students providing they have access to a good library.

Another source is in the history of the book's reception, from the first contemporary reviews (*D.H. Lawrence: The Critical Heritage*, ed. R.P. Draper, Routledge & Kegan Paul 1970) to the later critical assessments. Most academic critics of Lawrence discuss his intentions at length, often referring to his letters, and this may well be one area to explore with the help of critics. In particular, by looking closely at key passages in the novel which a number of critics have commented on in full, and which seem to embody the writer's intentions, students should be able to call on their own developing interpretations. It may be that during discussions some of the more difficult areas of intentionality will emerge. Does the reader really have much freedom to interpret the text if the writer's intentions, as embodied in the very structure and language of the novel, constrain the possible range of interpretations? Are students aware that as they grow as readers they may more easily see the writer's intentions implied in the text and that sometimes these may be at variance with stated intentions outside the text?

It's a rich area to explore, and a difficult one, and many teachers might rather avoid it, and concentrate more on what the students bring to the text as they struggle to make meaning.

This is what we shall concentrate on in the following section.

Revising the novel

RETURN TO THE READING JOURNAL

The sheer bulk of the novel often presents particular difficulties when students come to prepare for examinations. What particular study skills are needed to revise the novel for examinations? This question is complicated by a tension which faces teachers when they consider any text in the final run-up to examinations: how can guidance be given to students which does not undo the earlier work in developing a personal response to the texts? Two suggestions are offered here, the first of which is centred on extending personal response with some specific guidance, while the second is a structure devised by the teacher within which personal reflection can be clarified. These two techniques ought not be regarded as alternatives, but complementary.

A later series of journal reflections on notes made earlier during the first reading of the novel can be approached in several ways. Attempting to answer and extend comments on questions which were raised can produce important insights, and a return to the journal should imply a return to the text. In Jane's journal writing on the first section of *The Rainbow* quoted earlier for example, the question 'Why is Tom so sure (that his fate was coming)?' raises the issue of Lawrence's treatment of the process of choice-making in the novel and may well prompt reflection on Lawrence's treatment of how the characters understand what is happening to them. 'Why doesn't he make a move?' Jane wrote during her first reading. An answer informed by a knowledge of Tom and the whole book would now generate a greater understanding, individually articulated from a personal engagement.

As well as using questions and original confusions as starting-points for later critical reflections, the journal can be used as a source of personal patterns of interest or concern. Flow charts of common patterns of interest that recur through the journal can produce some exciting discoveries and important qualifications of what might have begun as simple observations. 'Lawrence writes about men and women separately – not as individuals,' noted Jane. Here is a potentially producive key theme to pursue throughout the journal, to present in diagrammatic form and annotate with comments in terms of differences and developments.

A third activity based on a return to the reading journal concerns a stepping back from the reading experience to encourage a monitoring of the learning that has been taking place. The questions to be asked when re-reading the journal in this way should be: What have I gained from reading this particular part of the book? What am I as a reader becoming aware of here? What do I seem to feel are the weaknesses of this book? What have been the strengths of this novel for me? Are there any other things I want to say about this novel that I feel to be my personal insights about the book? An approach which has encouraged the development of a sense of individual engagement with a novel will enable students finally to reflect on these questions with more ease than might be expected. The journal will provide detailed references with which these reflections can be explained in relation to the novel itself.

GUIDED RE-READING OF THE NOVEL

Return of the Native was about to be discussed for the last time before the exam in a last series of lessons. Issues which had arisen in earlier discussions of the novel had been noted by the teacher and these, together with other issues felt by the teacher to be important, formed the basis of a series of six worksheets issued before each lesson in which the six parts of the novel were to be discussed as though in serial form. Each worksheet was intended to pose questions which would form the basis of the lesson's work. Students brought to the lesson their individual comments on these questions.

The aim here was to provide some guidance to a re-reading of the novel in an attempt to crystalize personal responses that had been developed in earlier work on the book. So while directing the student to specific passages with specific concepts to consider, the questions were as open-ended as possible. The journal could be referred to in the preparation of answers to these questions. Here are the worksheets on 'Book First: The Three Women' and on 'Book Fourth: The Closed Door'.

Return of the Native: 'Book First: The Three Women'

1 What is the relation between people and the Heath in the first two chapters? Is it modulated in ch. 3?

2 What does the language reveal of Hardy's relation to his native Heath? Of working experience of furze cutter p. 11 and different knowledge of Celtic history, 'architectural demands' and 'organic' (Darwin) p. 20? What is the purpose of the language of p. 61?

3 Is the 'sky-backed pantomime of silhouettes', p. 21, melo-dramatic? Traditional and ballad-like? Abstract literary effect?

4 Is the indirect introduction of characters (Wildeve p. 29), the plot forbidding banns (p. 27), social values (p. 29), even the hint at plot development (foot of pp. 34/35), traditional life and style of natives (bonfire, ballad, dancing, superstitions), clumsy literary devices or traditional and dramatically (Shakespearean) appealing?

5 'The Three Women' of Book 1 are defined by their response to Wildeve. Compare their language and tone of their conversations (pp. 50ff and pp. 69ff). How does Hardy present Wildeve to the reader in each of these conversations?

6 How are passion, power (pp. 52, 72, 99, 106 – 'weapon') and position (foot p. 51, 90, 110) linked by Hardy's introductory Book?

7 In what ways could the chapter 'Queen of the Night' be describing the tensions and pressures upon nineteenth-century rural England, i.e. all the characters? In what qualities is Eustacia presented as being alienated from and connected with, customary rural life? Is she similar, or opposite, to Clym when he returns? Explain moral decline identified by chapter headings, from Perplexity to Dishonesty.

Return of the Native: 'Book Fourth: The Closed Door'

1 In *Woman in Love* Lawrence expressed the ideal relationship between man and wife as that of 'star polarity': 'two single equal stars balanced in conjunction' (p. 142, hardback edition). Hardy uses a similar metaphor of Clym and Eustacia (p. 245), but how has his image different implications?

2 How does Hardy imply, in his description of Clym the furze-cutter (p. 258), his gains and his losses in becoming a labourer?

3 Clym's French song as labourer prompts Eustacia's substitute for Paris in local 'gypsying'. Compare 'Paganism revived' (p. 266) with pessimism of loss of 'zest for existence in earlier civilizations' (p. 174).

4 Note the emotional and social confusion pointed out on p. 269. Can these moods be related to Clym's confusion and uncertainty?

5 Is it this uncertainty which is at the heart of the novel that leads Hardy to use the heath as anti-human (p. 283)?

6 Does the plot device of the money changing hands draw attention to, rather than cause, the fragility of relationships between the participants?

7 What feelings and thoughts are you left with after reading the rejection and death of Mrs Yeobright?

6

POETRY AND THE READER

Teaching poetry

Although A level was originally designed as a syllabus end-on to degree courses, it has been totally untouched by recent controversies over the aims and ideologies of English teaching in higher education (see p. 5). However, some of the new perspectives on reading are illuminating when we consider possible approaches to the teaching of poetry in the sixth form.

The growing interest in the reader as collaborating in the construction of meaning (see Tompkins 1980) helps us to focus more clearly on the stages of understanding and learning that students have to undertake (involving many kinds of mental activity from first-glance impressions through to reflective evaluation), and the importance of helping them to reflect on the processes of learning. The shift from the poem to reader inevitably involves us in speculation about how we perceive and understand, and avoids looking for some magical formula that will unlock any poem we read. There are no short cuts for coping with poetry, since every poem is distinctive, but, as with novels and plays, there are generic conventions and allusions which offer clues to the reader. But in the early part of a course time needs to be found for allowing students to read and explore poetry without the pressure to reach conclusions, so that there is scope for tentative first impressions, for swapping suggestions, for testing out meanings and so building their confidence as a group of readers who can share in the process of understanding and appreciation.

We need to think about appropriate tasks, too, since a recent report on A level literature (Dixon and Brown 1984), which we have already referred to, suggests that the mode of writing demanded by many A level questions has a backwash effect on the way poetry is read. Moreover, it is easy for students to underestimate the unique power of poetry to communicate, even when it is unfamiliar.

The way a poem is created is quite different from the ways of thinking and learning that dominate education. These are mainly discursive and sequential, constructed by rational argument so that we can use and apply patterns of logical thinking and analysis. Poetry by its nature is not discursive, but exists often in metaphorical and symbolic language; it can express feelings and thoughts as the poet perceives them, it accepts feelings and association which may surprise, puzzle, disconcert, or delight the reader. There is no analytical paradigm that we can apply to all poems, but that does not mean that the mind is inactive during reading. It is just that the reader needs time to dwell on the poet's words, to use her mind fully as she reads, drawing on experience of life as the poem prompts her to, responding to the new combination of words and rhythms. It is a very demanding attentiveness that the reader must bring to bear if meaning is to be constructed.

Much of our task in teaching, then, is to try to raise our students' consciousness of what poets do with language. This cannot be done in any systematic way, but early on in the course we can provide a series of lessons which might help attune the reader to the special nature of poetry and the kind of attention we must give it. Before considering stages of learning we want to sketch out some possible ways of encouraging students to become more aware of the power of poetry.

The suggestiveness of metaphor

Is it because most of the reading and writing in schools comes under the transactional umbrella that understanding metaphorical discourse seems to be such a problem? No doubt many of our students will be able to offer a working definition of the term, but then fail to notice in their reading of a poem that a metaphor offers evidence of the way the poet's mind works.

Here are short notes by students on an Edward Thomas poem,
'Cock-Crow':

> Out of the wood of thoughts that grows by night
> To be cut down by the sharp axe of light, –
> Out of the night, two cocks together crow,
> Cleaving the darkness with a silver blow:
> And bright before my eyes twin trumpeters stand,
> Heralds of splendour, one at either hand,
> Each facing each as in a coat of arms:
> The milkers lace their boots up at the farms.
>
> (Edward Thomas, 'Cock-Crow')

> The cocks are in the wood in the middle of the night.
> It starts to get lighter but the trees hide the light.
> Only when the wind blows the leaves a ray of
> sunlight cuts into the wood and brightens it up . . .
>
> (Dawn)

> The poem is about the woods at night . . . it is quiet
> and a good place for thinking. As the morning comes
> the light shines through the trees, showing things
> that seem out of place in the wood.
>
> (Carol)

Part of the trouble, perhaps, is that the students were asked to
write a commentary before they had had time to make notes or
ask questions (compare the section on 'Shared impressions', p.
117). They have skimmed for surface meanings and missed the
suggestiveness of 'wood of thoughts', with its allusion to a
landscape of the mind.

Reinforcing earlier work on metaphor may take time, but a
key concept can easily become blunt-edged if it is just part of
a checklist of things to watch out for, rather than an induce-
ment to think harder about what is being expressed.

There are other sources of confusion. Metaphors are often
subsumed under the heading of imagery, so convincing some
students that they are looking only for visual images. We try to
show them that metaphors are an expression of concentrated
and complex *thinking* going on in the poet's mind. So we avoid
the smart surface metaphor of the kind developed in poems
such as Craig Raine's 'The Window Cleaner', and prefer to use
poems which illustrate the complex network of thinking,

feeling, and meaning which co-exist in metaphorical language. To save space we quote extracts only, but, in practice, we would not want to take the lines out of their contexts. Teachers will have their own favourites, but this compilation has been used on a number of occasions:

> His brain was a whitewashed kitchen
> hung with texts, swept tidy
> as the body o' the kirk.
>
> (Seamus Heaney, 'The Other Side')
>
> The winter evening settles down
> With smells of steaks in passageways.
> Six o'clock.
> The burnt-out ends of smoky days.
>
> (T.S. Eliot, 'Preludes')
>
> The house has been far out at sea all night,
> The woods crashing through darkness, the
> booming hills,
> Winds stampeding the fields under the window
> Floundering black astride and blinding wet.
>
> (Ted Hughes, 'Wind')
>
> The yellow fog that rubs its back upon the
> window-panes,
> The yellow smoke that rubs its muzzle on the
> window-panes
> Licked its tongue into the corners of the evening,
> Lingered upon the pools that stand in drains,
> Let fall upon its back the soot that falls from
> chimneys,
> Slipped by the terrace, made a sudden leap,
> And seeing that it was a soft October night,
> Curled once about the house, and fell asleep.
>
> (T.S. Eliot, 'Prufrock')
>
> Why should I let the toad WORK
>   Squat on my life?
> Can't I use my wit as a pitchfork
>   And drive the brute off?
>
> Six days of the week it soils

With its sickening poison –
Just for paying a few bills!
That's out of proportion . . .

(Philip Larkin, 'Toads')

The day is turning ghost,
And scuttles from the kalendar in fits and furtively,
To join the anonymous host
Of those that throng oblivion; ceding his place,
maybe,
To one of like degree.

I part the fire-gnawed logs,
Rake forth the embers, spoil the busy flames, and lay
the ends
Upon the shining dogs;
Further and further from the nooks the twilight's
stride extends,
And beamless black impends.

(Thomas Hardy, 'A Commonplace Day')

There is always the danger that by concentrating on one feature
of poetry we shall be teaching students bad habits. Examiners
complain about 'mechanical' examination scripts, and they are
in part referring to the way some candidates just 'identify'
features and list them, rather than concentrate on the search for
meaning. By exploring metaphor within its context in a poem,
students may perceive some of the ways a poet exploits the full
range of expressiveness in language to convey thoughts and
feelings.

We would invite students to work in pairs, reading the poems
together and making brief notes:

1 Do the metaphors suggest an attitude towards the experience?
2 Are the metaphors central to the meaning, or a kind of
  decoration or elaboration?
3 Can the metaphors be explored in a number of ways (i.e.
  there is not just one correct meaning)?
4 Are the metaphors mainly visual, or do they appeal to other
  senses, or other kinds of perception?

First impressions

When we started teaching in the sixth form, it took us a long time to learn to take things more slowly. In our eagerness to elicit responses and comments from students we often failed to recognize their problems with what they were reading. We should have remembered our own sense of insecurity in the sixth form, and our attempts to avoid answering questions from the teacher because we seemed to be working at a much simpler level.

We now know much more about the value of group work, thanks to the work of Barnes, Britton, Dixon, and so on, although as yet there is remarkably little written on sixth form group work. We will now describe three different approaches to shared work in the early stages of the course: active comprehensions, shared impressions, and shared questions, before considering the potential of individual notes.

Active comprehension

The ideas in this section have been developed from the work of the Schools Council (1979), *The Effective Use of Reading*. The project coined the term DARTs which stands for Directed Activities Relating to Texts. The principle of these activities is that they direct students towards certain features of the text but allow room for exploration of those features in an open-ended and often indirect way. DARTs have provided very good approaches to group work in preparation for full class discussion, having demanded some personal engagement with the text in a form which is obviously tentative and exploratory. Some examples of DARTs used in the preparation for class discussion of texts can be indicated here by several different kinds of activities we have devised in exploring with students the meanings of two poems by Ted Hughes, 'Full Moon and Little Frieda' (*Wodwo*) and 'Earth-Moon' (the final poem in *Moonbells*: Chatto 1978).

The work on 'Full Moon' required the recording of Hughes reading the poem (*The Poet Speaks*: Argo PLP 1085) and big sheets of card plus felt-tipped pens of two colours per pair of students. This recording is an extended version of the text published in *Wodwo* and is printed in *Ted Hughes: A Bibliography 1946–1980* by Keith Sagar and Stephen Tabor

(Mansell 1983). It should be emphasized that the process of 'making something' on a sheet of card to show the full class when reporting back is, of course, only providing a focus for group discussion at this stage, although with exploratory labelling the products can provide an interesting display alongside a copy of the text. Here is what six groups were asked to do after listening twice to the reading by Hughes with a copy of the text in front of them, and with the reading available for a re-run as needed:

1 Choosing a part of the poem, or the poem as a whole, make a diagram to chart the changes in rhythm and intensity of expression in the reading.
2 This is a free verse poem, yet spacing on the page is clearly carefully controlled. Choose a section of the poem to show the effect of length of lines and line endings by using signs instead of words as you rewrite those lines.
3 Find as many images of balancing and tension as you can, and represent them with cartoon images, linking them with lines and any annotations necessary to suggest their inter-relationships.
4 Make a picture to show what you think is going on in the last two lines of the *Wodwo* text.
5 Draw cartoon images representing what stays in your mind after hearing the final section which was eventually cut from the poem. Show any links with earlier images in the *Wodwo* text.
6 Choose one aspect of your response that can be represented in a line of polarity, for example delight–disgust; eerie–comforting; warm–cold; tense–relaxed. Plot the six *Wodwo* stanzas on a scale of -5 to $+5$ then plot the additional section of the poem.

The following tasks required a little prior arrangement with the Art and Textiles Departments so that students could be sent there to paint and to explore fabrics. Only the text was available for these activities, plus the card and pens:

1 Prepare a reading of the poem using your three voices, singly or together at times, to convey your reading of the text.
2 Make a final list of five questions which you would genuinely like to ask your friends about the poem to help you under-stand it.

3 Make a painting of the earth-moon as the man in the poem first sees it.

4 In six frames of a cartoon show the changing meaning of the moon for you in the poem. You may wish to caption each frame.

5 Devise a tableau of three moments in the poem.

6 Design the trophy so as to demonstrate its meaning for you at the end of the poem.

7 No emotions are referred to in this poem. Devise a flow chart to map the rising emotional changes of the character in the poem.

8 If this poem were a fable what would its moral be? Sum it up in one sentence.

A group of teachers working on activity 7 produced the diagram below which is worth reproducing here as a possible further teaching resource.

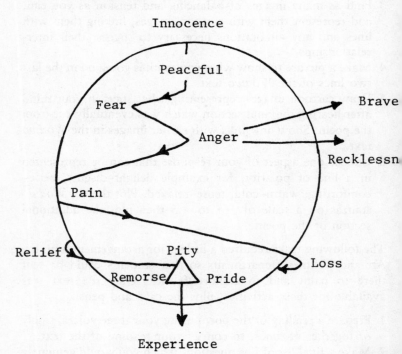

The writer's stance cartoon: 'View of a Pig'

'It weighed, they said, as much as three men.'

'I thumped it without feeling remorse.'

'. . . one feels guilty . . .'

'Once I ran at a fair in the noise.'

'Pigs must have hot blood . . .
They eat cinders, dead cats.'

'They were going to scald it,
Scald it and scour it like a doorstep.'

A Graffiti Board:

3 *Esther's Tomcat* ◄── (decapitation) ──► 4 *Hawk Roosting*

'Grallochs odd dogs on the quiet,
Will take the head clean off your
simple pullet.'
(Violent language represented
in this different approach.)

'There is no sophistry in my body:
My manners are tearing off heads —'
(Self preservation. Violent instinct
to kill for survival.)

1 *Thrushes*
'More coiled steel than living.'

(indestructibility)

'Dark a poised deadly eye . . .
Triggered to stirrings beyond sense —
With a start, a bounce, a stab . . .'

'How loud and above what
Furious spaces of fire do the distracting devils
Orgy and hosannah, under what wilderness
Of black silent waters weep.'

'Nothing but a bounce and stab
And a ravening second.'

'That hungers the shark's mouth
the blood-smell
even to a leak of its own
Side and devouring of itself . . .'

(mechanistic
self-preservation)

2 *Snowdrop*
'Brutal as the stars of this month
Her pale head heavy as metal'
(metallic/mechanistic imagery)

6 *The Jaguar*
'Over the cage floor
the horizons come.'

5 *Pike*
'. . . silhouette of submarine delicacy.'
(Paradoxical — delicacy and shock tactics.)
'Past nightfall I dared not cast . . .
For what might move, for what eye might move.
(Both endings have the suggestion of what is
lurking in the depths of man's subconscious.)

Further suggestions for activities relating to texts can be found in our chapter 'Creative responses in the sixth form' (Gifford and Brown 1983). Additional suggestions for the teaching of poetry may also be found in Terry Gifford's chapter 'Working with poetry' (in Blatchford 1986). But here it may be helpful to give two more examples of DARTs in detail.

THE WRITER'S STANCE CARTOON

Students had read two poems by Ted Hughes, 'The Hawk in the Rain' and 'View of a Pig'. They were asked to imagine a circle as representing the subject matter of the poem and a dot to represent the writer of the poem. In the six frames of a cartoon they were asked to trace the change in the writer's stance towards the content of his poem. Extreme objectivity would be represented by the dot far outside the circle; extreme involvement would be represented by the dot at the centre of the circle. A quotation should caption each frame. The diagram shows one example from a pair of sixth form students.

MAKING A GRAFFITI BOARD

Students were asked to choose and then sequence six poems to introduce readers to the central issues in Ted Hughes' *Selected Poems 1957-1967*. Quotation and connotation were to be used to create a graffiti board from which new readers could be given a talk about the texts.

Shared impressions

As with the suggestions for work on Shakespeare, we see collaboration as one of the ways of helping students to feel less insecure when tackling difficult poems. In introducing a group of students to the poems of John Donne we invited them, in pairs, to prepare a reading of one of the poems aloud, followed by shared first impressions which they were to jot down. Where they had difficulties they could either ask questions for other groups to discuss, or spend time themselves trying to find answers. Here is one example:

The Sunne Rising

1   Busie old foole, unruly Sunne,
     Why dost thou thus,

Through windowes, and through curtaines call
on us?
Must to thy motions lovers seasons run?
   Sawcy pedantique wretch, goe chide
   Late schoole boyes and sowre prentices,
    Goe tell Court-huntsmen, that the King will
ride,
   Call countrey ants to harvest offices;
Love, all alike, no season knowes, nor clyme,
Nor houres, dayes, moneths, which are the
rags of time.

2   Thy beames, so reverend, and strong
      Why shouldst thou thinke?
I could eclipse and cloud them with a winke,
But that I would not lose her sight so long:
   If her eyes have not blinded thine,
   Looke, and to morrow late, tell mee,
    Whether both the India's of spice and Myne
   Be where thou leftst them, or lie here with
mee.
Aske for those Kings whom thou saw'st
yesterday,
And thou shalt heare, All here in one bed
lay.

3   She'is all States, and all Princes, I,
      Nothing else is.
Princes doe but play us; compar'd to this,
All honor's mimique; All wealth alchimie.
   Thou sunne art halfe as happy'as wee,
   In that the world's contracted thus;
Thine age askes ease, and since thy duties
bee
To warme the world, that's done in warming
us.
Shine here to us, and thou art every where;
This bed thy center is, these walls, thy
spheare.

A1 (1) I can easily imagine Donne sitting up in bed shouting
and shaking his fist at the sun which is acting like an
old busy body.

B1   Why 'unruly'? Is the stress on 'thus'?

B2   'Lovers seasons' – He's already magnified the time – why?

A2   He seems more playful – 'sawcy pedantique wretch' but why 'pedantique'? Now the sun is a court official. Does Donne despise the farm workers (I suppose 'country ants' means that?). What were class distinctions like in those days – is this an in-joke?

A3   I like the last two lines – they could be said very quietly, except for the throw away 'rags'. Does the mood change too fast from anger, to commands, sarcasm (country ants) to the calmness at end?

It's encouraging to see how much the students have gained from reading the poem aloud: from Angela's first vivid demonstration of the opening, to questions about stress ('thus') and tone ('He seems more playful', 'they could be said very quietly', 'Does the mood change too fast?'). Neither girl wanted to try to answer the other's questions but said that they had directed them to the rest of the group for discussion. They also admitted that some of these notes were written after a fair amount of chat, hence the rather cryptic comment:

B2   He's already magnified the time.

and the clear grasp of lines 5–9: 'the sun is a court official', 'sarcasm (country ants)'. There are two questions about the meaning of words – 'unruly' and 'pedantique' (the text was not annotated), and a rather strange question at the end – 'Does the mood change too fast?' – which shows the beginning of a judgement being made.

A4 (2) More playful. I like the exaggerated joke in l.3 – eclipsing with a Wink, but not wanting to lose her sight.

B3   More scorn in idea of the lover's eyes 'blinding the sun'. Is this first mention of his wife, lover?

B4   'India of Myne' – I can't work that out. Why 'tomorrow late'?

A5   More playful exaggeration – all the kings in one bed?

Once again the struggle to find a satisfactory reading aloud of the poem has given the two girls the confidence to comment on the tone: A4 – 'more playful'; B3 – 'more scorn'; A5 – 'playful exaggeration'. The aside in B3 – 'Is this the first mention of his wife, lover?' – suggests a slight uneasiness, and the question about 'India of Myne' could be resolved by a brief reference to seventeenth-century spelling. A5 is a too literal reading of lines 19 and 20, although 'exaggeration' suggests the students are close to understanding the line.

A6 (3)   Still exaggeration, but simpler words 'Nothing else is'.

B5   He's casting aside honour and wealth. 'Play' – does it mean 'act'?

A7   'Thou sunne' – now he's pitying it – 'Half as happy', 'thine age' and 'Old foole' back in 1.

A8   First lines – most exaggerated. Is this before Galileo?

B6   The bed becomes the centre of the universe? No more anger, but he's still haughty?

A2   Is it all to impress the woman? Or to get rid of his anger?

B7   Parts seem very romantic – 'She is all states . . .' but parts are comic, too? I like the character of the writer.

Yet again the notes on tone are impressive: B6 – 'No more anger, but he's still haughty?' The final two comments throw open the discussion about the poet's purpose and show that one of them, at least, likes the 'character of the writer'.

There is space here to show the notes of only one pair of students, but by looking at the other five sets of notes the teacher was in a much better position to see where help was needed about meaning, background, and interpretation. Not all the questions the students had directed at the other pairs were looking for final answers, and the tentative nature of some of the judgements – 'he's still haughty?', 'Is it all to impress the woman?' – give scope for re-thinking and second thoughts. (The notes were kept in their files, so that they could be referred to and revised at later readings.)

Shared questions

This approach involves a kind of role-play. Pairs of students were invited to read poems aloud, but this time they were to formulate the one or two central questions they would like to ask the poet if he were present. On this occasion the poet was Blake, and we looked at two of the *Songs of Experience*, 'The Tyger' and 'The Sick Rose'. Some years later John Brown had the chance to involve more students, when he was preparing a workshop for a group of Belfast teachers. On that occasion he also asked teachers to jot down the central questions they would like to discuss with students. The examples which follow are taken from all these sources.

The Tyger

Tyger! Tyger! burning bright
In the forests of the night,
What immortal hand or eye
Could frame thy fearful symmetry?

In what distant deeps or skies
Burnt the fire of thine eyes?
On what wings dare he aspire?
What the hand dare sieze the fire?

And what shoulder, & what art,
Could twist the sinews of thy heart?
And when thy heart began to beat,
What dread hand? & what dread feet?

What the hammer? what the chain?
In what furnace was thy brain?
What the anvil? what dread grasp
Dare its deadly terrors clasp?

When the stars threw down their spears
And water'd heaven with their tears,
Did he smile his work to see?
Did he who made the Lamb make thee?

Tyger! Tyger! burning bright
In the forests of the night,
What immortal hand or eye,
Dare frame thy fearful symmetry?

The task was not as straightforward as had been assumed. By confining pairs of readers to two central questions these students were being expected to go through the early stages of understanding and response too hurriedly. So some of the questions addressed to Blake were still very basic, implying a first or second reading only:

1 Did you see an actual live tiger? Where?
2 What is the link between the blacksmith and the tiger?

3 Which is the most important question in the poem?

Perhaps the first question could be partly answered by looking at the facsimile of the original, where the tiger depicted there looks anything but real (cf. *Songs of Innocence and of Experience*, Introduction by Sir G. Keynes, Oxford University Press 1970). Question 3 aroused a heated but worthwhile discussion. A further set of questions addressed to Blake probed more deeply:

4 Why do you just ask questions? Are you expecting us to try to answer them?
5 Although you ask 'Who made the tiger?' do you have a ready answer?
6 Are you pleased with the poem? We feel it's unfinished, and the meaning hidden. Did you revise the poem?

We can refer to an earlier draft of the poem to show that Blake did revise and that the poem we're familiar with is a final draft:

THE TYGER

1 Tyger Tyger burning bright
In the forests of the night
what immortal hand & eye
or
Could frame thy fearful symmetry
Dare

What the anvil What *the arm*
arm
grasp
clasp
dread grasp
Could its deadly terrors *clasp*
Dare *grasp*
clasp

2 *In what* distant deeps or skies
Burnt in
Burnt the fire of thine eyes
The cruel
On what wings dare he aspire
What the hand dare seize the fire

6 Tyger Tyger burning bright
In the forests of the night
What immortal hand & eye
Dare *form* thy fearful symmetry
frame

3 And what shoulder &
what art
Could twist the sinews
of thy heart
And when thy heart
began to beat
What dread hand &
what dread feet

Could fetch it from
the furnace deep
And in thy horrid ribs
dare steep
In the well of
sanguine woe
In what clay & in
what mould
Were thy eyes of fury
rolld

4 *What* the hammer
what the chain
Where where
In what furnace was
thy brain

[*On the opposite*
page]

Burnt in distant deeps
or skies
The cruel fire of thine
eyes
Could heart descend
or wings aspire
What the hand dare
sieze the fire

5 3 And *did he laugh* his
work to see
dare he *smile*
laugh
What the shoulder
what the knee
ankle

4 *Did* he who made the
lamb make thee
Dare

1 When the stars threw
down their spears

2 And waterd heaven
with their tears

Questions 4 and 5 take us to the heart of the poem, as does
another one, more in the form of a statement:

7 We think you know the answers to your questions and
you are just trying to make your readers think.

If we compare these seven questions to a group that students
wrote for their peers, we notice that the latter seem to be
modelled, perhaps understandably, on a typical comprehension
exercise:

1 Do you find Blake's use of imagery effective?
2 Comment on the meaning of
   a) aspire
   b) sirens
   c) immortal.
3 Why does Blake use animal imagery?

4 Do you find that Stanza 5 flows on from 4?

5 What sort of creation is the tiger depicted as?

Finally, if we look at a few of the questions which teachers said they would like to ask their students, they start at a level well beyond the first impression stage:

1 What is Blake's idea of God? Gentle? Wrathful? Both?

2 How do you interpret the second two lines of verse 5 and in what sense is this the key to the poem?

3 What is the significance of the forge imagery – 'hammer', 'chain', 'anvil'?

The terms of these questions are nearer the orthodox examination ones, with the stress on 'idea', 'key', and 'significance'. Only two of the teachers' questions were aimed at an early stage of reading:

4 What do you expect to find in a poem with this name?

5 After hearing the title were you surprised by the content or wording of the poem in any way? What did you expect?

What can we learn from these groups of questions? First, that we need to think very carefully about what stage of reading our students have reached. If they are at a first impression stage we should avoid questions that attempt to find hidden or elusive meanings, because these may steer them one way only. We need to find more open questions which do not imply an assumption about the poem, as above. Part of the problem for many teachers is that it is virtually impossible to remember what it was like when they first read the poem, because it is so familiar.

Let us see if the questions on 'The Sick Rose' produce similar groups.

The Sick Rose

O ROSE, thou art sick!
    The invisible worm,
That flies in the night,
    In the howling storm,

Has found out thy bed
    Of crimson joy;
And his dark secret love
    Does thy life destroy.

The central ones that students wanted to put to the author this time implied considerable familiarity with the poem:

1 Is a sexual interpretation of the poem more valid than a religious one?
2 Do you mean us to think about how other poets have used the symbol of a rose in their poetry?
3 We'd like you to explain why the worm which flies is invisible, and what you mean by 'dark, secret love'.

That last crux troubled many students, as we see in the questions they presented to their peers:

1 What significance does the worm have? Why is it invisible?
2 Why does the writer use the word 'flies' in verse 1?
3 Is this poem simply about the decay of a flower?

Certainly these are the kinds of thoughts that might come to us after a first reading, and we'd want to tease them out. Some of the teachers' questions are less didactic than those on 'The Tyger' and the first two might be useful at an early stage of reading:

1 Why do you think the poet addresses the rose – 'O Rose, thou art sick'?
2 How can roses become sick? What is the cause and nature of the sickness?

Perhaps what all these questions help us to consider are whether we are trying too soon to shift students towards our own more experienced perceptions before they have had time to grapple with the poem at the frontiers of their own consciousness and understanding. The power of reading and comprehension is unpredictable and untidy, and students often undervalue their own rough and tentative impressions and thoughts and turn too soon to external and more authoritative interpretations. The individual search for meaning is not a straightforward, linear progression because the mind may choose to look back to check earlier impressions, may make sudden imaginative leaps and may behave in unforeseen ways.

Individual notes

Students' or teachers' questions like those in the last section will almost certainly promote discussion, but we need to be aware that imposed questions can also channel lines of speculation and enquiry towards a predetermined end. Offering a question which is based on a firmly held view of a poem (the teachers' or examiners') may constrain too early an inexperienced reader's perceptions and even prevent her realizing that she thinks and feels differently about the poem.

So there is certainly a place for private jottings by individuals which allows them to explore meaning in their own terms, however inexperienced and limited these may be. In the following example students were invited to record their early explorations of Blake's 'The Sick Rose'.

Some in the group did not start with jottings about details or images but tried to subordinate these in an attempt to express an overall first impression. Probably none of us would care to adjudicate on which of these approaches is more helpful in the early stages of reading, but clearly some of the readers found it helpful to look at the poem as a whole:

> 'The Sick Rose' gives an impression of incredible over-ripeness, similar in this respect to 'The Ode to Autumn' by Keats. This feeling of over-ripeness, a rose past its prime, almost makes one feel quite ill especially with the introduction of a worm which I imagine to be a maggot.

> I find this very frightening; the rose is absolutely powerless, and cannot even recognise its destructor – 'the invisible worm'. It gives one the idea that nothing is safe – innocence will inevitably be destroyed. Very terrifying.

> There is no remorse for the Rose. The feeling I get is that the writer thinks the rose is pathetic, as if beyond pity. Blake knows the rose for its own destruction.

> The poem suggests a kind of malignant suffering. The worm eats away at the rose, like a cancer, having found a valuable place from which to start.

Blake's poem has induced strong feelings in these readers and already there are differing attitudes towards the 'rose'. We remember that as young teachers we were over-anxious about students misreading a poem if left on their own, and in a somewhat dogmatic way we directed discussions in the way we wanted. Now we are convinced, having offered students more scope, and looked at the results, that if students are to develop their own powers of perception they should be trusted to explore meanings on their own and in groups.

The kinds of students we worried about were those who seemed content with literal, surface impressions, as here:

> On first reading the poem I thought the Rose had got greenfly and this is what a lot of roses suffer from, but I was puzzled by the mention of the invisible flying worm.

> There are too many insects which kill roses, yet it seems too easy to believe that Blake is just telling us of the Rose's parasites.

The *Gardeners' Question Time* approach is amplified in both cases by misgivings, but the literal approach is continued in notes on the worm:

> Caterpillar is the natural enemy of the rose, so why a worm?

> The worm could be the worm which causes the rose to lose its petals as it occurs in a howling storm.

> Perhaps Blake uses the word 'worm' to convey how much he dislikes the wind for doing what it does, just as often we call people we dislike 'little worm', etc.

One of the students, on the other hand, tried to link the 'worm' with 'its dark secret love', keeping closer to the author's emphasis:

> It is only the worm which is actually evil and he seems to feed on the Rose's weaknesses. The only thing that does not fit into this context, however, is still the word love. I fail to see how the worm can love this rose yet still destroy her deliberately.

Other students developed similar thoughts but then explored more fully the connotations of 'destroys' (rather than verbs like 'maintains' or 'creates' which we normally associate with love).

> The most powerful word is 'destroy'. It concluded the poem with a sharp suddenness, and implies all sorts of evil. This is reinforced by the use of 'dark secret love' which has very sinister undertones.

> Love is the subject of 'destroy' and is therefore not the pure happy feeling of the songs of innocence, but a selfish, over-powering lust.

We also get the implication that the worm gets enjoyment out of injuring the rose. This is a very sinister, evil enjoyment.

The most penetrating comments come from a student who expressed a dawning realization that the love Blake speaks of is 'cruel' in the 'pursuit of its goal' and who perceived something important about the shape of the poem and the build-up of emotion:

> What ends the rose's life is 'love'. Thus we view love as the cruel merciless body who is opposed to beauty. The impression I have due to love being called the destroyer of beauty (rather than its creator) is very strange . . . love is portrayed as an independent agent, destroying all before it, even beauty, in pursuit of its goal. Love's methods are regarded with increased displeasure and disquiet for the rose. The very last point is emphasised by the 'wailing' nature of the poem, for there is essentially only one simple long sentence which rises to a peak of emotion with the final word 'destroy'. The actual emotion is a combination of grieving pity for the rose and growing outrage at the cruelty of the invisible worm's love.

These remarkable insights are expressed as they develop, from the hesitation of 'very strange' to the more confident 'increased displeasure' and finally to the more assured 'growing outrage'. This student's construction of the poem is based on attentiveness to the full connotations of the poet's words but expressed in his own language.

These notes on Blake were written by a group of students in the lower sixth who all produced more than one side of impressions. The range of insights, as we've seen, are from surface ones to others more penetrating, but they are all worth keeping by the students, to return to at a later stage in the course, when the focus will have shifted almost inevitably to trying to see Blake's poems as a whole, in preparation for the examination.

In the last three sections of this chapter problems of misreadings and misunderstandings have been raised, and it is here that the teacher's intervention becomes important. This can be in the form of questions added to the students' notes, or by drawing attention to parts of the poem that may have been ignored. The best help a teacher can give at this stage is to try to analyse the students' learning (not the poem!) and comment on it, and to help provide an atmosphere of concentration and receptivity. As we said earlier, there are no procedures or systems for unravelling a poem, but we can try to help students to prepare their minds for a new experience in language. They will need help in distinguishing between what a consensus of experienced readers identify as 'facts' in the poem (meanings of words, identifying the context of the poem and its speaker, and so on) and those places where the individual reader seems to have more freedom to construct meaning. But there may well be disagreements at an early stage about what students perceive as 'facts', and airing these will be important.

Beyond first impressions

The stage beyond first impressions is always more difficult because there is a temptation to categorize and generalize too soon. The search for a unifying theme or motif can often result in such broad concepts (nature, love, evil, and so on) that the integrity of a poem is reduced to extracted images and lines which serve merely to illustrate these abstractions. Such work will be highly appropriate shortly before the A level exams, because of the kinds of questions often set (see Chapter 7), but during these early stages the pressure to subordinate details to the whole can often lead students to borrow knowledge and perspectives before they have the confidence to handle language at a more concentrated level. The kind of commentary found in 'guides' or handbooks is often of this more general kind and we would want to warn students away from it.

The search for themes is tempting, seeming to offer the reader a way of standing back from the particular and giving some coherence to what may be, at this stage, very confused impressions. But uncertainties, unanswered questions, and initial problems can easily become subsumed under general headings, and parts of a poem which don't easily relate to extracted themes are ignored or forgotten. The following suggestions, which have been compiled from many different sources, are ways of helping students to grow in confidence in areas in which they have control. The writing involved is still mainly in the form of notes.

EDITORS' NOTES

Many school and examination editions include notes on poems, and selecting appropriate editions for A level students is a difficult task. By using notes from two or three editions, the teacher can invite students to think about these difficulties: which notes are the most helpful? Which the least? After referring to notes, do you still have problems or questions about the poem? How has the editor introduced background material, if at all? Does he refer to earlier drafts or editions? What are the function of such notes – exposition, interpretation, comparison, and so on? After a class session along these lines, students can be asked in pairs to prepare notes on one or two of the poems they have been studying for fellow students or next year's group. This kind of work can be specially interesting when studying modern poems because, on the whole, editions of Hughes, Larkin, Hardy, and so on are not annotated.

Footnotes: compare editors' notes in *Songs and Sonets of John Donne* (ed. T. Redpath, Methuen 1957), *Metaphysical Poems of the Seventeenth Century* (ed. H.J.C. Grierson, Oxford University Press 1921), and *Poems of John Donne* (Penguin 1950).

SPEECH AND SONG

This is a simple scheme to introduce students to scansion, without too much technical encumbrance. By looking at poems which are close to speech or song, we can ask students to concentrate on stress or accents, and on rhythm and intonation in the poems they are studying. Here are some starting-points:

Poems closer to speech:

'The Wood Pile'   – Robert Frost
'Neutral Tones'   – Thomas Hardy
'The Tea Shop'   – Ezra Pound

Poems closer to song:

'Sweetest Love'   – John Donne
'The Lamb'   – William Blake
'The North Ship' – Philip Larkin

The task can be assigned to groups of two or three students, mixing the two groups of poems:

1 Can they find a simple way of testing the claim that some of the poems in this selection seem closer to speech and some to song?

2 How do we normally stress or assert words in speech (it may, of course, be different from how they are spelt: for example 'polished' has only two syllables when spoken)?

3 Is this different from the way words are stressed in songs?

4 What do you understand by regular and irregular rhythm?

5 What effect does the rhyme scheme have on the way the poem is spoken aloud?

6 Use / for stress or accent; X for unstressed word or syllable.

It may be helpful for the teacher to have examples of poems where the rhythm is so dominating that it is difficult for the reader (or listener) to concentrate on meaning; for example 'The Hounds of Spring' (Swinburne) and poems where the rhythm seems to help to make the reader (or listener) more receptive; for example 'A Deep-Sworn Vow' (W.B. Yeats).

This workshop is designed to help students to find simple ways of discussing rhythm and stress without overloading them with technical jargon. Having explored rhythm and stress, the groups can be invited to say what effect these seem to have on meaning and feeling; for example, does the rhythm throw the stress on particular words? Does the rhythm raise expectations in the reader and then thwart them (or satisfy them)? Does the rhythm seem to keep control of the emotion or let it run away?

We have deliberately avoided referring to metre, that is the regular pattern of stress found in different forms of poetry, since it seems more important at this stage to focus on rhythm, that is on the actual movement of the words in the poem as they are spoken. For intonation, simple markings can be agreed for the rise and fall of the voice. The findings of each group of students can be shared and tested, with any misunderstandings thrown up. Then groups can return to the set poems they were originally studying to apply some of their findings, using the categories of 'speech' and 'songs' as reference points. Do they help readers in preparing the poems for further reading aloud?

READERS' SCRIPTS

As a follow-up, students can be invited to prepare copies of the poems they are studying for others to use in a public reading (the poems can be typed out or copied on to a large sheet of paper). This will be a kind of informal test of their own initial grasp of the poem. In addition to the signs for stressed and unstressed words/syllables previously mentioned, a mark for a pause (|) is useful, along with other signs or notes to show the pace of the ideal reading, volume, intonation, etc. Students can invent their own system of signs for reading more slowly or quickly.

The following examples show how students marked their poems:

Subdued throughout

Neutral tones

We stóod by a pónd that wínter dáy,
And the sún was whíte, as though chídden of Gód,

More emphasis here, but quieter

And a féw leáves láy on the stárving sód;   Monotone?
– Théy had fállen from an aśh, and were gráy.

Yoúr eýes on mé were as eýes that róve
Over tédious ríddles of yéars ago;
And somé wórds pláyed between uś tó and fŕo
– On which lóst the moŕe by our lóve.

More bitter

The smíle on your moúth was the deádest thíng
Alíve enough to have streńgth to díe;
And a grín of bítterness swépt thereby   Slightly faster
– Like an óminous bírd a-wíng . . .

More emphasis here

Sincé thén, keén leśsons that lóve decéives,
And wríngs with wŕong, have sháped to mé   very quiet and subdued

Gradual slowing down

Yoúr fáce, and the Gód-cuŕst sún, and a trée,
And a pónd edǵed with gráyish leáves.

(Thomas Hardy)

Pied Beauty

Quite fast

Glóry be to Gód for dáppled thíngs –
For skíes of coúple-colóur as a brínded cow;
For rosé-móles all in stípple upon tróut that swím;
Freśh-fírecóal chéstnut-faĺls.; fińches' wíngs;
Lańdscape plótted and piéced – fóld, fállow, and
  plóugh;
And all trádes, their geár and táckle and tŕim.   Slower

Stress 'all'

Aĺl thíngs coúnter, oríginal, spáre, stránge;

Keep balance

Whatever is fićkle, fréckled (whó knows how?) Quieter
With swíft, slow; sweét, sóur; adázzle, dím;

Hé fathers-fórth whose beáuty is paśt chánge:

Praíse hím.

(Gerard Manley Hopkins)

Poetry, music, sound effects

First, in Shakespeare's plays there are many songs which composers in different periods have reinterpreted in their own musical idiom. There are, for example, versions of 'O Mistress Mine' by Morley, Quilter, and Warlock. Students who go regularly to RSC productions will be aware of the way that the company regularly commissions new settings of the songs to suit particular productions, while at other times it uses traditional tunes. Clearly there is a rich field to explore here, even for students with limited musical skills. Many poems have inspired composers to set them to music, and there are recordings of many of them:

Benjamin Britten	– poems of Donne, Tennyson, Keats, Hardy, Owen, Auden, Blake
Ivor Gurney	– poems of Shakespeare, Clare, Edward Thomas
Gerald Finzi	– poems of Hardy (over fifty in five song cycles)
George Butterworth	– poems of Housman
Madeleine Dring	– poems of Betjeman
John Dankworth	– poems of Auden
Armstrong Gibb	– poems of Walter de la Mare
Ralph Vaughan Williams	– poems of Whitman, Stevenson, Blake, Housman

A selection of recordings of these can be played and discussed in terms of their mood and interpretation. Does the music offer a fresh insight into the poem? Has the composer exposed the rhythmic structure of the poem? What are the key moments in the musical version (that is change of key, swelling or softening of melody, discordant accompaniment, for example)? Do they differ from the key moments in a sympathetic reading? Keen musicians in the group may wish to try to set some of the poems they are studying to simple guitar, keyboard, wind, or brass accompaniment. Perhaps there is an opportunity to see if such work could be linked to their A level music work?

Second, for students who are studying music or have the interest, it may be interesting to try to find appropriate music as a background to a public reading of the poems they are studying. Extracts from symphonies, tone poems, jazz, for example, may suit the rhythm or mood of particular sections of a poem so that an edited tape can be made (not all parts of a poem need to have a musical accompaniment). Does pastoral music (e.g. Vaughan Williams' Fifth Symphony, Delius, Bax, Moeran, and so on) suit the mood of pastoral poetry? Does the music of the age offer an appropriate musical background to contemporary poetry? For example:

Byrd, Dowland, Purcell	– seventeenth-century poetry
Bach, Telemann, Vivaldi,	
Handel, Arne	– eighteenth-century poetry
Berlioz, Beethoven	– Romantic poetry

Four-track reel-to-reel recorders allow the music to be pre-recorded on a separate track and then the reading on a different track, for playing back together, or readings can be made over the recorded music.

Some of the most interesting results came from a group of students who were studying the poems of T.S. Eliot. After a fairly simple tape to accompany 'Prelude', they produced a very atmospheric tape for 'Triumphal March' (including percussion) and finally an ambitious and impressive tape for 'The Waste Land'. The choice of music was wide – jazz and dance tunes of the 1920s, Mahler, Elgar, Charles Ives, Wagner, Debussy, and Strauss. The group discussions about the choice of music inevitably explored meaning and interpretation.

Simple sound effects or percussion may also be used to accompany poems. The RSC have experimented over the past few years with elaborate sound effects in some of their productions, and radio and television have produced similar readings. Percussion is, of course, particularly useful in any discussion of rhythm and stress.

The aim in all of these sessions is to promote informal talk about the poems, and to try to extend students' appreciation of the poems without setting formal critical essays. Brief notes on why a group chose the particular extracts or sound effects will provide a permanent record for other A level groups in subsequent years.

Poetry, slides and videos

If there are students who are keen on photography or there is a sixth form photographic club, it is not difficult for students to make a set of slides as appropriate background to a reading of poems (with or without musical or sound accompaniment). All kinds of photographs and paintings can be used as slides – landscapes, portraits, abstracts, and so on. Other departments in the school or college may have suitable slides for loan, and stocks of slides can generally be made available for students to browse through. Very simple but strong and dramatic slides can be made up by buying white transparencies and applying patterns or words with felt-tipped pens or overhead projector pens. The potential for drawing attention to colour or tone in a series of poems is impressive; similarly the highlighting of words or phrases is effective in a series of slides bordered or backgrounded with colour. There are many anthologies which use photographs or paintings alongside poems (e.g. 'Worlds') and, of course, Ted Hughes combines poems with photographs or paintings in 'Remains of Elmet', 'River', 'Under the North Star', and 'Flowers and Insects'. Recently groups of teachers in the Midlands and Yorkshire have been making short videos, presenting visual metaphors and sound effects as background to a reading of selected poems. Those groups who have access to good editing suites are at an advantage here, but there is scope for students who are taking both A Level Literature and A Level Communication Studies to experiment.

In any work with slides or videos, it seems to us important that students keep a detailed journal of all stages of the work, not only to record group decisions, but also to ensure that those involved are thinking hard about the processes of linking words to visual images. Are they being faithful to the meaning as they perceive it in the poems?

Anthology

After students have read and explored a number of poems by one writer, invite them to select three or four poems for inclusion in an anthology, or as an introduction to the poet's work. The anthology could have different purposes depending, of course, on which parts are on the syllabus, for example, a collection of nature poems, a contemporary anthology, political poems, poems of war, or satire. This might be the students' first steps in looking for significant links between poems, in terms of subject matter, attitude, ways of exploring experience, mood, and so on. Students can then be asked to write a short introduction (one or two sides), which again may have a variety of functions; for example, as an introduction for a new reader, or as a commentary on why these particular poems have been selected.

The introductions would then be available when the teacher wants to spend time discussing the problems of writing about groups of poems, rather than just one. There are anthologies where the writers themselves have written the introduction (e.g. 'Worlds') and these could be contrasted to other editors' introductions (e.g. in A. Alvarez's *The New Poetry*, Penguin 1962).

Poetry writing and students' journals

If we are serious in wishing to widen the range of writing demanded by an A level English course, the writing of poetry must have a place on such a course, just as the students' journals will contain a range of tentative, exploratory forms of writing. There are times when the writing of poetry has a natural place in close relationship with the study of poetry and times when it should have a place quite separate from the work on set texts.

PERSONAL JOURNALS AND PUBLIC WORKSHOPS

If poetry is an intensive way of exploring thoughts and feelings through the precise manipulation of language we should be encouraging students to be using this as a tool to make such explorations regularly for themselves in their personal journals, jotting down notes, images and ideas, drafting and redrafting. As will be seen later (Chapter 8), some Alternative A level syllabuses make provision for this writing to contribute towards the students' final grades. Some syllabuses, indeed, demand some creative writing. Whether this is the case or not, it is our belief that every student can gain from writing poetry themselves as a means of personal imaginative exploration, playfully or painfully, with wicked wit or serious searching at different times.

The regular testing of work-in-progress on readers in a group workshop can, with tactful supportiveness from the workshop leader, show that the discipline of textural criticism can be a useful tool in developing each other's writing. (Note the distinction in Chapter 8, 'Alternative A levels', between private cathartic and audience-oriented writing. The former is not brought to the 'Workshop for readers' responses'. The latter is brought on the assumption that it may be redrafted on the basis of readers' suggestions about parts of the poems that might be reconsidered by the author. But the author is controller of her text and decides what changes to try out later as a result of the workshop.) Workshops need take place for only one lesson each half-term, but from them will come, inevitably in our experience, poems of impressive quality which ought to find a life in print for a wider audience within the school, college, local, or national poetry magazines.

WRITING IN RELATION TO READING

The writing of poetry can be used, not only as a way of producing interesting poems from students, but as a way of exploring texts. Here are four examples of different ways of doing this:

1 The challenge of the problem: Discussion of Larkin's 'The Whitsun Weddings' had led to a spirited disagreement as to whether Larkin took a patronizing view of ordinary people. So we went away to write a poem that observed someone doing something without our being condescending in tone. Could we do it? Is all observation bound to be patronizing to a degree?

2 The interpretation of the sequel: The mystery at the heart of Paul Muldoon's poem 'Why Brownlee Left' left us puzzled. We explored our personal intuitions in a sequel written in the voice of Brownlee which began 'I am writing this . . .'

3 Literary stylistics: How does the sonnet work? What can or cannot be written in this form? How does a chorus alter the stanzas of a ballad? How free is free verse? Does the apparently spontaneous form of D.H. Lawrence's 'The Bat', for example, have random line-lengths? Write a poem about an experience of an animal in this form, but set it out in two different ways. See the different effects created and the number of decisions to be made by a writer of 'free' verse.

Some of these can be linked to the induction programme discussed in Chapter 3.

4 Response to a theme: It might seem obvious, but how often do we find it done? How often are students asked to explore their own reflections on the central theme of a poem or poet by writing a poem which either replies directly to the poet or bounces out of the poet's subject matter in a personal experience of it, or reflection on it? We had been listening to a tape of Gillian Clarke reading her 'Letter from a Far Country'. This poem evokes the lives of several generations of women in rural Wales. We went away and wrote our own poems about the experiences of women as we perceived them.

Reading poetry ought to lead to the need to produce poetry. Most writers read other writers to generate and reinvigorate their own creativity. Most people are writers; that is, most people are capable of using writing as a way of constructing meanings about their physical and imaginative lives. Most people are capable, sooner or later, of producing something of surprising felicity, even if it is only a line or a phrase of real originality or insight. This does not stop at the end of primary schooling, or at the age of 16, or at the end of the A level course. Students ought to know this. There are an increasing number of writers' workshops in the community and this is a movement with which students should see themselves connected. Education needs to take people beyond simply being consumers of literature into the modest (or ambitious) roles of producers of literature.

Teaching the longer poem

Some examination boards still require as compulsory the study of a longer poem in a separate part of an examination paper. These set texts tend to be as varied as *The Rape of the Lock* or *Absalom and Achitophel*, *The Ancient Mariner* or *The Prelude*, Books I and II, *Peter Grimes* or *The Eve of St Agnes*, *The Wreck of the Deutschland* or *The Waste Land*. Only the latter ever seems to represent the twentieth century. Doubtless the examiners are eager to vary this list and simply haven't got around to reading the latest examples of the genre. In fifty years' time we might see on their list Terry Harrison's *V* and Liz Lockhead's *The Grimm Sisters*.

The problems encountered in teaching the long poem are in many ways exaggerations of tensions in the heart of teaching any poetry: how to grasp the overall patterning in relation to identifiable turning-points; abstracting themes at the expense of the poetry working as poetry; tracing imagery out of its contextualized meaning; recognizing, as a contemporary reader might, the difference between literary conventions as the norm and conventions as ironic play at different moments in the poem.

The potentialities offered by these poems are, however, unique to the longer poem: room for the development of areas of personal interest; opportunities for group work on different sections; potential for dramatic performance; possibilities for exploration of literary stylistics by adding 'newly discovered' sections as formal exercises in students' writing. Some examples of what we have in mind are best given in relation to individual texts.

AREAS OF INDIVIDUAL INTEREST: *THE PRELUDE*, BOOKS I AND II

After an initial reading of the text during which students were asked to note key moments that interested them, we compared these moments and returned to the couplet which seemed to launch many of them:

> Fair seed-time had my soul, and I grew up
> Foster'd alike by beauty and by fear.

Almost every word here contains a concept which can be explored throughout the text: Wordsworth's view of himself as a 'natural' seed; the meaning of 'soul' growing up but 'foster'd'; the counterbalance of experience of 'beauty' and 'fear'. Such concepts were taken back to the individually chosen passages and students then grouped passages relating to their own area of interest. They negotiated individual essay titles, then tested out interpretations and theses on the class in brief seminars before eventually submitting their essays.

GROUP WORK ON *PETER GRIMES*

(Card and felt-tipped pens available.)

1 Select moments of description that reflect his psychological state and be prepared to explain these to the class.

2 Select quotations to help us understand the interrelationship between his social encounters and his isolation.
3 Chart the changes in the writer's moral stance through the poems.
4 List as many different functions of the couplet as you can find.
5 Diagrammatically represent the narrative structure of the poem.
6 Make a flow chart of the psychological change of Peter Grimes using numbered lines of the poem.

DRAMATIC PERFORMANCE OF *THE ANCIENT MARINER*

The text was divided into seven sections and each section allocated to a pair of students who were to ask two questions of the class about two mysteries in their section before performing a reading that gave their own tentative answer through performance. When we came together we therefore had a fragmented thought-provoking performance. Questions varied from 'What are the slimey things?' to 'What has the telling of the story done to the Mariner to make him "a wiser and a sadder man"?'

DR ARBUTHNOT'S ESSAY OF CRITICISM ON POPE'S *THE RAPE OF THE LOCK*

Bill Greenwell has described how he prepared his students for anticipated difficulties in their forthcoming journey through *The Waste Land* by devising the Sybil Project by which, through their own writing, they would be introduced to

> the concepts of symbolism, dramatic monologue, the compression and fragmentation of imagery and meaning – the literary equivalents of montage and collage, on which Graham (the Art teacher sharing the group and studio space) worked simultaneously.
>
> (Adams and Hopkins 1981)

Form was not our first concern in teaching *The Rape of the Lock*, although its enjoyment was evident as students read out their favourite couplets after an initial reading. After sorting out just what Pope was doing in the poem and reading his *Essay on Criticism* (selecting couplets which might be applied to *Rape*)

and *An Epistle to Dr Arbuthnot* (selecting best and worst
couplets) students had some familiarity with the Augustan
couplet and its epigrammatic potential. It was time to turn out
one of their own. Pairs worked on producing one couplet that
commented upon *The Rape of the Lock* in as perfect a form and
with as epigrammatic a force as they could muster. These were
then edited together as though by Dr Arbuthnot, borrowing
Pope's lines from *An Essay on Criticism* which had given us an
opening and a model. The resulting composite Epistle began:

> Tis hard to say if greater want of skill
> Appear in writing or in judging ill;
> The gilded wit of society and pen
> Can draw the narrow lines of women and men.
> Our Alex wrote his thoughts in flowery verse
> Then Terry made us read it: Tis a curse!

This went on to develop an awareness of both sexism and post-
Augustan wit:

> Oh Belinda, who controls the game?
> Without your hair, will it be the same?
> Betty, what this show of sorrow?
> Hair today and gone tomorrow!

7

PREPARING FOR THE FINAL
EXAMINATION

This chapter is in two sections: the first takes a critical look at
the nature of A level questions, and then examines a series of
questions and suggests ways of helping students to recognize the
opportunities and constraints. (The questions are on *Hamlet*,
The Rainbow, and the poetry of Ted Hughes.) The second
section offers practical suggestions for planning revision for the
final examinations.

A critical look at A level questions

The questions and tasks set in the orthodox A level English
Literature examinations have no public model in literary
criticism. Quite simply the constraints imposed by the mode of
examining – the severe time limit, the absence of the books
studied, the unseen questions and the one-off occasion – divorce
the candidates' writing from any of the normal conditions for
reviewing or commenting on books (even if we include dead-
lines and restricted column space).

It comes as no surprise, therefore, to notice that the Alternative A levels which have been developed over the past ten to
fifteen years have been replacing these formal examination
constraints with conditions more appropriate for writing about
books, for example coursework elements, which allow students
to negotiate the tasks with their teachers and to write in their
own time, and open-book examinations, which allow copies of

the books to be present and therefore demand changes in the kind of questions asked.

Apart from the examination constraints, what makes the A level tasks so unlike those that critics perform?

THE SELF-CONTAINED TEXT

We'll restrict our comments to Shakespeare's plays set at A level because their de-contextualization is most striking. Although teachers often discuss the conventions of the Elizabethan theatre with their students, and take them to see productions, there is rarely any reference in A level questions to the fact that Shakespeare's texts are in reality playscripts which have be reinterpreted by every generation of producers and actors. Critics of widely differing ideologies – Christian, Marxist, Absurdist, Feminist, for example – have constructed their own versions of these scripts.

If we examine the history of the popularity of Shakespeare's plays we discover that some virtually disappeared from theatres during the nineteenth century, only to reappear in striking productions in the 1920s and 1930s, for example, *Measure for Measure* and *Troilus and Cressida*.

The differences in stage (and film) performances are sometimes extreme. Olivier's version of *Henry V*, made at the end of the Second World War and dedicated to the Parachute regiment, presented a heroic young king, resolute and unswerving. Ian Holm's characterization at Stratford in the 1960s made Henry a reluctant hero, so that his shrug of the shoulders after the rallying speech before Harfleur suggested that he found the role of kingship a burden. In Kenneth Branagh's interpretation at Stratford in 1984, the king almost had a nervous collapse after Agincourt and had to be physically supported by Exeter. If we were to turn to the great tragic roles, such as Hamlet and Lear, we would find even more extreme differences in interpretation. Looking carefully for support in the script for such interpretations would be a purposeful task for students.

However, questions of diverse theatrical interpretation appear to have little place at A level. No guidance is offered to teachers about how to prepare students for the Shakespeare paper, except for the implicit message in the kinds of questions set. Rarely are students invited to refer to productions they have seen, and there are no references to different historical and cultural contexts. What conclusions can be drawn?

It seems that the plays have to be studied as if they were each self-contained with universal meanings, despite the vast changes in social, moral, religious, and political conditions. Do we have to set aside insights gained from feminist critics about the way Ophelia's character has been portrayed over the centuries (cf. Chapter 4, p. 64)? As readers and viewers, teachers know full well that there are no absolute interpretations of the plays. How much longer will we have to put up with a tradition of examining literature which seems to be based on the first Honours English paper set at Oxford University in 1896, when the following questions appeared:

> Has the term 'Political Justice' any meaning applicable to the tragedy of *King Lear*?

> Write an essay on the character of Henry IV as represented by Shakespeare in different plays.

> (Potter 1937)

Questions similar to these can be found on any recent A level papers. Critical theories about the nature of literature, its means of production, its place in different cultures, and the relative merits of pluralist interpretations, which have been informing courses and modes of assessment in higher education for some years, seem to have made no inroads into the senior literature examination in schools.

SENSE OF PURPOSE AND SENSE OF AUDIENCE

Critics make meanings from books according to their own beliefs: an Anglican will look for Christian assumptions, a Marxist will reinterpret in the light of Elizabethan power relations. They write for an educated audience and their purpose is often to persuade readers that their interpretations merit consideration. Many critics attempt to 'correct' earlier writers, but expect to take part in a series of polemical debates, especially in a pluralist society such as ours.

In contrast, many of the questions set at A level do not invite an individual student to write from the standpoint of her own developing and, in most cases, still immature interpretations of the play. Too many questions demand a form of detached debate or argument which is not the best form for expressing a sensitive critical commentary (Dixon and Brown 1984: 12–14). Often questions are at such a high level of abstraction that the student is unable to choose and select material in her own terms.

'The core of the play is the conflict between good and evil.' Is this a fair comment on *Hamlet*?

Such an abstract question seems to imply absolute concepts of 'good' and 'evil', rather than the problematic view of human nature to be found in *Hamlet*. What notions of 'good' and 'evil' does the young student bring to the play? Is Hamlet's misogyny a sign of goodness or his preoccupation with death? What the question seems to demand is a kind of intellectual sophistication that abstracts the reader or viewer from her own experiences of the play. And what is implied by 'fair' in the question? How many times will the talismatic words 'good' and 'evil' be used by candidates without reference to their individual perceptions? A question to be avoided at all costs! Let us take another:

'Enthralling though many speeches and scenes are in themselves, the play does not form a coherent whole.' Examine this view of *Hamlet*.

Whatever does 'a coherent whole' mean? Students who have seen intelligent and coherent productions are unlikely to want to spend much time trying to discuss propositions like this, which are abstract and aesthetic, placing any human aspect of the play at a great distance. Do we read books and plays because they 'form a coherent whole'?

PERSONAL RESPONSE

When examination boards outline their aims, they always refer to notions of assessing the candidates' 'response to literature' (cf. p. 4), and yet, in practice, they produce questions like the ones above. How do examiners expect candidates to show any evidence of personal response when in the very wording of questions there seems to be no reference to individual reader or thinker? Global concepts like 'good', 'evil', and 'coherent whole' are bound to alienate the young student from her own immature grasp of a play like *Hamlet*. Instead, if she attempts to answer, she will masquerade and pretend that she has succeeded in interpreting the play in the given terms.

THE LANGUAGE OF CRITICISM

There appears to be no consensus among the examination boards about the kinds of language which may enable or constrain students in their writing. Some questions invite commentary on specific parts of a text while others are dressed in general and abstract terms, as above. Doesn't the use of generalizations in a question attract an answer at a similar level of abstraction? Take this example:

> What does *King Lear* imply about the nature of evil? Substantiate your argument by reference to characters and plot, and by quotation.

This is one of the questions referred to by Frances Stevens (1970), where she deems this to be an 'interesting and fair question'. We cannot agree. The assumption, like the first *Hamlet* question, is that the play is mainly about philosophical problems. Students have to consider the play as a whole as a manifestation of Shakespeare's ideas about evil. This is very different from assuming that different readers will draw different conclusions about what *they* perceive as 'the nature of evil' as Shakespeare presents it. It is not surprising that so many of the answers printed by Dr Stevens were encumbered with generalizations, polarized categories, and schematic moral patterns.

A common feature of the language of examination questions is its impersonality:

> 'Browning's great subject is the soul's development.' Discuss.

Note that the student is not addressed in this typical format, except implicitly in the peremptory 'Discuss'. What is the source of the quotation, its authority? What on earth is meant by 'the soul's development'? If the student wants to disagree does she have to make any reference to that empty phrase? (Try using this quotation to discuss 'Encounter by Night' by Robert Browning.)

We also object to questions like these because they do not reflect good teaching. A good examination system should surely reflect good teaching, not superimpose alien terms and concepts. Here is another example, even more confusing:

'Wordsworth varies his blank verse admirably to suit his different purposes.' Discuss.

The student is directed to an area of uncertainty, 'purposes', but as a reader she will surely want to refer to the *effects* of the poem. The reader's role in interpreting meaning seems to be totally ignored in that question. There is little room for manoeuvre in that word 'Discuss'.

Inviting students to write on literary texts seems to be an underdeveloped or difficult art for examiners, with few signs of any change, despite recent research on language and radical new approaches in literary criticism. Why have all of us who have taught A level not been more vigilant or vocal in our criticism of the tasks set in the examinations?

WHAT IS A GOOD QUESTION?

Is there any agreement among teachers and examiners about what they mean by a 'good' question? An examiner may define it in terms of a question which will produce a wide range of answers, discriminating between stronger and weaker candidates. Most of the teachers we've talked to have different criteria in mind. They would like to see questions which are genuinely addressed to a student audience, expressed in clear, unambiguous language, and which invite students to focus on central issues, instead of confining them to peripheral areas. As one teacher said:

> The ideal question should provide the opportunity for a student to write on what she has found interesting in her set books.

The following questions are from the Australian HSC papers:

The Go-Between

Looking back at her relationship with Ted, Miriam says, 'Our love was a beautiful thing. There was nothing mean or sordid in it, was there? and nothing that could possibly hurt anyone?' How would you answer her question?

Laurie Lee

'An autobiography is just an exercise in egotism for the writer.' What does Laurie Lee's autobiography, *Cider with*

Rosie, have to offer you the reader?

Both questions address the student as someone who has an individual stance and voice, and they are nearer the kinds of tasks a teacher might negotiate with a group of students, recognizing that there is a crucial relationship between the reader and the book. All too often the questions at A level put all the attention on the text, as if the acts of reading, responding, and thinking were passive instead of productive.

As a final note to this section we should like to recommend a provocative and thoughtful article by an A level teacher, Roy Goddard (1985), 'Beyond the literary heritage: Meeting the needs in English at 16–19'. His radical scrutiny of A level includes much that we agree with, both on structure and questions, especially his analysis of questions as in induction into University English discourse:

> The primary function of the traditional A level course is that of *selection* and in serving this function it sets its face firmly against the human needs of the majority of students who take A level.

Ways of coping with A level questions

We would strongly recommend that any teacher dissatisfied with the orthodox A level should attempt to join an Alternative scheme. There are promising initiatives from some of the boards, who are now making what were originally pilot or restricted alternatives open to all (see Chapter 8). However, by far the largest number of candidates are entered for the orthodox examinations, and in the final stages of preparation they will need help in recognizing the opportunities and constraints in the form and language of questions, and also plenty of practice in planning answers.

Most questions, as we have seen, come in the form of an assertion or proposition, with instructions to 'discuss', 'consider', 'explain'. How much or little freedom there is within these frameworks is open to interpretation. Is it inevitable that the structure for most answers will be in the form of a debate, because that is a very restricted form for writing about literature? Are the terms of the question directing the candidate to general issues at a distance from the experience of reading and response? How does a student keep in touch with his experience as a reader as he answers such questions?

Our first set of questions (drawn from across the boards) is on *Hamlet*. As we have already criticized the language and constraints of some of these questions, it seems only right to start with those.

a) 'The core of the play is the conflict between good and evil.' Is this a fair comment on *Hamlet*?

The problem here for the student is to relate those abstract terms 'good' and 'evil' to her own reading and understanding of the play, so that they can be redefined locally in selected scenes and speeches. The candidate needs to be warned against trying to juggle with those abstractions, and to avoid looking for neat patterns in the play. Instead, if the student is still disturbed by aspects of the play which simply cannot be described in those polarized terms, there is scope for some personal exploration. For example there are many occasions when Hamlet's behaviour may seem destructive to the reader – his treatment of Ophelia, his harsh words to his mother, his lack of remorse over the killing of Polonius. Can the burden of revenge be discussed in terms of 'good' and 'evil'? By discussing some of these aspects of Hamlet the student can avoid making the play a simple morality, with a 'good' prince opposed to a corrupt King and Court. How will the student want to include relevant comments on Ophelia and Gertrude, on Horatio, on Fortinbras?

To sum up: the candidate has to find ways of translating the abstractions into moments of theatre (see Chapter 4) by locating the conflict in particular scenes and speeches so that there is scope for more personal involvement. Students who find problems with aspects of Hamlet's behaviour have a chance to make these relevant to the question.

b) 'Enthralling though many speeches and scenes are in themselves, the play does not form a coherent whole.' Examine this view of *Hamlet*.

Behind this question is an aesthetic view of art which can be traced back to Kantian philosophy! It places value in the organic design of a play, implying some kind of unity into which all aspects of the play neatly fit. This kind of aesthetic preoccupation appears to undervalue the human content of the play.

How does the student try to bridge this gap? In the fleeting time available, it may be useful for the candidate to recall briefly a production which one hopes was a satisfying experience, and begin to account for the satisfaction. Was she aware of central issues which seemed to be reflected in different parts of the play, for example contrasting attitudes to revenge, the development of Hamlet as he tries to cope with avenging his father's murder, strong contrasts between Hamlet's father and his uncle, different kinds of loyalty, conflict between public respect and inner corruption, and so on? In other words the student should be able to select some elements which could be discussed in terms of *design*, as perceived by the audience. There may also be aspects of the play which the student finds puzzling or unsatisfactory, for example Horatio's untrue account of events at the end, Hamlet's preoccupation with sexual betrayal, Fortinbras' role at the end. If there are personal misgivings, the student may be able to refer to them *in her own terms* as signs of incoherence or unevenness.

To sum up: the student will have to look for some kind of pattern or design in order to conform to the question, but she can select details from the play and try to keep in touch with her experience of a production. Problem areas can be discussed as perceptions of dislocation or of conflicting effects. It's important for the student to retain her individual voice here.

c) Discuss the view that we learn the most important things about Hamlet from his soliloquies.

Here the student is directed to particular parts of the play, although there is scope for reference beyond the soliloquies. The temptation may be to treat the soliloquies in chronological sequence, summarize them and try to extract insights about Hamlet. It is important here for the candidate to take stock quickly of those scenes in the play where she was impressed or surprised by Hamlet's behaviour, and note aspects of his character which do not preoccupy him in his soliloquies, for example his treatment of Ophelia, the killing of Polonius, his behaviour at the funeral of Ophelia. What are the contradictions between the private and public Hamlet? The soliloquies need to be recalled in their contexts; for example, Hamlet seems to be at his most determined ('My thoughts be bloody') when he is under arrest, bound for England, and therefore totally ineffective.

To sum up: there is an opportunity here, with careful selection, to explore some of the most vivid parts of the play, but not confine all attention to the soliloquies. The candidate could make a personal statement, qualifying the 'we' in the question.

d)   'But I have that within which passeth show,
        These but the trappings and the suits of woe.'
Explore some of the ways in which Shakespeare in *Hamlet* stresses the differences between what is real and what is false or assured.

The student has to recognize quickly that this question demands two things: the differences between what is 'real' and 'false' need to be made specific and local so that she can comment in a personal way, but there are also matters of dramatic technique and method to be explored. It would have been more realistic to ask how the audience is made more aware of the differences, because the question implies authorial intentions. There is the danger that the abstract words – 'real', 'false' – will distance the student from what happens on stage, and a personal interpretation has to be made at the start, to avoid constant repetition of the two words. 'Real', in any case, is ambiguous – real to whom, other characters on stage or the audience? Is self-deception 'real'? Apart from obvious distinctions between the public and private lives in Elsinore, are there tensions in Hamlet's soliloquies between what is 'real' and what is 'false'?

To sum up: another question using general categories, and so the student must be able to offer a personal interpretation and move back to the play, re-creating and dwelling on different dramatic effects, for example, irony, change of scene, soliloquy, echoes from other scenes, and so on.

e) Write an essay on revenge as a tragic theme in *Hamlet*.

Impersonal wording again with a whiff of danger in the phrase 'tragic theme'. Is there some way in which revenge can be discussed as it manifests itself in the play other than as part of the tragedy of Hamlet, for example in Laertes' behaviour? Is the examiner fishing for references to the conventions of revenge tragedy? The student has to avoid the temptation of writing too distantly about different attitudes to revenge, but try to keep close to the drama on stage, and her own perceptions. How does she react to Hamlet's refusal to kill Claudius at prayer only because he wants to find an occasion when the king is indulging in his pleasures? Does Hamlet obey the Ghost's injunctions, which include leaving his mother 'to heaven'? What problems do we have, as a modern audience, with revenge in *Hamlet*? Do we find anything to admire in Hamlet's treatment of Rosencrantz and Guildenstern? Hamlet is 'weary' of life before he is given the task of revenge – is that another tragic theme?

QUESTIONS ON *THE RAINBOW*

For the next set of questions, on *The Rainbow* by D.H. Lawrence, we offer brief comments on the opportunities and constraints, as we see them.

a) 'Lawrence's achievement lies in his vivid presentation of physical and emotional experience. He is less effective when he tries to explain these experiences.' Discuss.

An extremely difficult task without the text to hand. The student may be able to argue that it is the *range* of experience which is so impressive, but to be strictly relevant she needs to be able to refer in detail to Lawrence's language. 'Presentation' and 'explanation' are blunt terms for trying to describe the different ways Lawrence presents experience, so there may be scope for a more subtle or refined commentary. A question to be avoided, because of the absence of the text.

b) 'The three generations in *The Rainbow* achieve different levels and kinds of fulfilment.' Discuss and compare the difficulties and preoccupations of any two individuals from different generations.

With no reference to the author and his art, this question seems to focus on 'content', with no apparent opening for the student's response to the individuals chosen. In a simpler form this kind of 'character' question is common at GCSE level. We would advise students to refer both to Lawrence's sympathies and antipathies, and to their own, since otherwise answers to this could rely too heavily on narration and summary. Students who have read Leavis on the novel will recognize his critical concerns in the quoted statement. On the surface, a highly impersonal question which the student needs to penetrate with their own responsive language.

c) '*The Rainbow* is a great social novel, showing how each generation is faced with different cultural choices and pressures.' Discuss.

This shifts the student into different territory and there is scope here for a well-read candidate to refer to other novels under the heading of 'social', but, at the same time, it is easy to overlook the author's art because it is not referred to explicitly. It is to be hoped that, in discussing the dimensions of a social novel, the student will ensure that the writer's stance and ideology are referred to. Those students we referred to earlier (p. 98), who found Lawrence's portrayal of Will too emphatic in its disapproval, would be able to make relevant use of their comments here. The main problem is that there is so much to discuss here, if each generation is to be discussed in some detail, and the danger is that the student's responses will be squeezed out. Careful selection of episodes (illustrating the 'choices') will be needed.

d) How does Lawrence's use of symbolism help you to evaluate the characters in *The Rainbow*?

An uncommon direct address to the candidate, with the opportunity for a personal evaluation of both the characters and the author. But it is not an easy question because it may elicit a well-rehearsed sequence or scheme of symbols. The students need to have the confidence to present their own personal commentaries on the symbolism, because an author's 'use' of symbols depends on the reader's collaboration. The young reader may be more persuaded by some of the symbolic scenes (for example, stacking the sheaves, in the cathedral, on the barge) rather than Lawrence's overall design in which he introduces symbols of doorways, arches, pillars. The terms of the question invite a personal evaluation, and other novels could be briefly referred to.

e) 'He made the days – whether intense or ordinary – of his characters' lives more important than the themes of the novel.' Discuss.

Here is a statement with which the student may wish to agree or disagree. It's quite possible to argue that it is in the depiction of his characters' lives that the author's themes become apparent. The problem with the question is to avoid too much description or narration in discussing whichever 'days' the student selects. If the text were available the question would offer other possibilities, but at least there is scope for a personal choice of scenes and events for commentary. The student needs to keep the second half of the question in mind, and may want to write briefly about the nature of 'themes', and how far some of these are constructed by the reader or author, or both. It may be wise to refer to a range of characters (rather than concentrate on one or two) and to some of the longer scenes, such as the wedding, which can be seen as pivotal in the design of the novel.

f) 'The strength of Lawrence as a novelist lies in his ability to portray human conflict.' Examine this statement in relation to *The Rainbow*.

The problem with questions of this sort, which isolate one of the author's strengths, is to know how far you can go in referring to other qualities. There are certainly key scenes in each generation where Lawrence portrays 'conflict', so the student could make her own selection and comment on these. But implied in the question is a doubt about Lawrence's presentation of concord or harmony, and we would argue that it would be relevant to refer to some of those scenes (for example the reunion of Tom and his wife) where Lawrence's strengths as a novelist are also manifest. There is scope for discussing what the student sees as the key issues in the novel, such as the struggle for individual fulfilment, and the inevitability, therefore, of human conflict. As with the previous question we would advise students to refer to a range of 'conflicts', perhaps considering each generation, and not just focus on parent-child, or man and woman. The student has the freedom to focus on scenes which were found powerful and memorable, and these may well include Ursula's struggles at school, as well as her turbulent relationship with Skebensky.

QUESTIONS ON THE POETRY OF TED HUGHES

a) Examine Hughes' achievement as a poet of nature.

Much may depend here on the student's experience of other

poetry of nature, because it is an umbrella term capable of different definitions and interpretations. Hughes' development as a poet embraces different attitudes towards nature, and a student who has been reading some of his recent poetry (not available in *Selected Poems*) will be able to refer to some of these distinctions. The question, apart from its imperative 'examine', seems to offer some scope for personal commentary and interpretation. References to other nineteenth- and twentieth-century 'poets of nature', albeit brief and strictly relevant, may help the student to demonstrate Hughes' achievement. Without the text available, detached comments on Hughes' description may prove difficult, but the term 'examine' is, we suppose, sufficiently neutral for the candidate to express any sense of dissatisfaction with aspects of Hughes' poetry, although the emphasis should be on a sense of its achievement. It could be difficult to answer if the student has not read much other poetry of nature, but perhaps the greatest danger is to discuss attitudes rather than comment on poetic evocations.

b) 'Hughes' universe lacks human sympathy.' Discuss with close reference to any poems you wish to choose.

There is a generous invitation here to refer to 'any poems' and the student who has been reading more recent volumes of Hughes' poetry may be able to refer to his compassion in the elegies in *Moortown*, for example, in order to broaden her answer. There seems to be an implicit demand to define Hughes' 'universe' in some way, and the student has the freedom to range across his poetry but try to avoid some of the early catch-phrases and labels that tend to minimize Hughes' qualities as a poet. The problem may be in the words 'with close reference', because although the student may have read widely, to be faithful to the demands of the question her comments may have to be confined to those poems in *Selected Poems* she has been preparing for the examination. The role of the poet himself may be worth exploring, since his presence is often the exclusive human one in many of his poems. As a human being he clearly feels sympathy, although not necessarily sympathy for humans. This ambiguity in the question invites explorations in two directions.

c) 'The contemporary poet does not claim any special powers of insight.' Have you found any 'special powers of insight' in Hughes? Refer closely to the poetry to justify your answer.

This question is rather ambiguous, since it is a generalization about many poets. However it is there, it seems, in its negative form merely to invite the student to comment on its positive side, the recognition of 'special powers of insight'. 'Insight' may refer to many different aspects – the self-awareness of the poet, his insight into the human or natural world, his creation of myths, and it seems to allow the student considerable freedom to explore the poetry of Hughes in her own way. Reference to other contemporary poets can be relevant, especially perhaps to those who write about social and political concerns. The student needs to remind herself of the final part of the question, and refer to those poems she knows best in detail.

d) 'Poems have a certain wisdom. They know something special.' (Hughes)
Discuss with close reference to three or four poems from this selection.

It's not often that the authorship of a quotation is acknowledged. If students haven't met these words before, they may have to enter into a discussion about the relationship between author and poet. The danger is in the word 'wisdom', and out of context, Hughes appears to be saying that there is something extractable from a poem, a message, and students may be tempted to select poems that they think they can summarize or paraphrase. The 'wisdom' in a poem is inseparable from the particular combination of words and images, so that a quotation like the one above (unless it is already familiar) could mislead students, especially those not so confident.

Students who are familiar with Hughes' book *Poetry in the Making* (Faber 1967) should be able to recognize the drift of his meaning, and sense the 'special' way in which poems work upon readers.

To sum up: In this chapter we have been suggesting that candidates minimize the odds against them in the examination by doing four things:

1 Avoid the worst questions, those formulated totally in abstractions that do not invite a personal discussion of the text's possibilities for interpretation.

2 To treat questions as opportunities to explore a holistic sense

of the achievements and limitations of the text on an individual reader – to develop a personal thesis in other words, which the teaching should have been nurturing and sharpening (cf. p. 158).

3 To answer the questions by centering on potent experiences of the text: moments of theatre where meanings are made in all their subtlety in a performance, poems which have been the source of interesting reflection, passages which have been significant to the reader's rather than teacher's interpretation of the text.

4 To draw on comparisons with wider reading that help clarify notions such as 'revenge tragedy' or 'poet of nature' in a manner which is prepared, if necessary, to challenge the assumptions of the question.

We hope that teaching methods which have allowed room for the personal development of students as readers and writers will have catered for 'the human needs of the majority of students' as well as the potential university students.

Final revision

All courses which lead in the direction of some form of examination of set texts allow time at the end for something called 'revision'. What exactly happens during revision? For many teachers it is a student-oriented word assuming the re-reading of texts, notes, and essays. But what is the role of the teacher during this time? How much guidance can or should be given and in what form? Some of the previous chapters have ended rather uneasily in the hope that approaches encouraging personal response, explorative, tentative engagements with texts, and varied modes of discourse in both creative and critical forms, will not be undermined by the need to confront the demands of the examiners in their forms of questions and conventions of answers. The central challenge is to find methods of guiding the final preparation for the examination in ways that maintain a fresh individuality of perception and the articulation of those perceptions. The following practical suggestions are a form of compromise that we have come to find workable over many years of facing this challenge.

A PERSONAL THESIS

After a period of journal reflections, group discussions, and perhaps latterly in the course, disagreeing with published critical statements, each student can have a sense of what is different about their own view of a set text from others in the group. This may be located in their personal readings of specific passages and it may also take the form of some ideas about the text as a whole. In re-reading their journals, notes, and essays, students can be asked to move towards making a statement of their 'personal thesis' about the text. This should not be longer than two paragraphs and should sum up the strengths and weaknesses of the text as the individual student sees them. The kind of writing we have in mind here is well illustrated by a journal reflection made late in the course by a student writing after a discussion of Chapter 19 of *The Grapes of Wrath*:

> Steinbeck realises that the stage is set for revolt, and assumes that it will come one day. He seems sure that he is right, and indeed the seeds of revolt are certainly present and growing, but, in the end, is he biased? Can the people really overcome their oppression? He sees from the inside as his writing of conversation shows. But the revolution is *not* inevitable. The poverty is short term, not long term as in other countries where revolution occurred. It seems to be wishful thinking on Steinbeck's part – a wish for an uprising.

Furthermore, footnotes should be added to the personal statement indicating key passages the student would point to in elaboration of the argument. Additional footnotes should then be appended of at least two statements by, or about, the writer that could be used in developing this personal thesis.

This may sound ambitious, but even at its simplest – a personal list of the text's strengths and weaknesses – it can give students confidence in their individual possession of a text in the face of oncoming exam panic. Practice is then needed in finding an appropriate way of making some of these points in answering specific questions. Examiners want an answer to the question asked rather than a question which might have been prepared for, but they also do not want to see the school's or the teacher's answer reproduced at different levels by the group of candidates. Individual engagement and a sustained argument is what they say they are looking for. The 'personal thesis' should provide a basis for this kind of answer.

GUIDING RE-READING WITH A WORKSHEET

At the end of our chapter on the novel (p. 105) we gave an example of one attempt to guide a re-reading of *The Return of the Native* towards key passages for those students who were still in need of a way into re-reading the novel for revision. It raises questions about themes and relationships between passages in order to provoke personal insights of a high level of subtlety from those students who can pursue them. Of course, the questions are leading, but it is important that they are open-ended too.

This form of breaking down the text when time is short can be applied to texts other than novels, of course. It is really an answer to the anxiety of 'Where do I start?' when confronted with the revision stage of the course. The worksheet of open-ended questions on specific passages of the text can provide an entry-point and total coverage of as 'elusive' a text as *Waiting for Godot* for example.

This can be fun, and serious points about serialization and reader-expectations in that intimate form of relationship with the public might be provoked by this final worksheet on *The Return of the Native*, which focuses on the final 'Book', which Hardy calls 'Aftercourses':

At last!	*Return of the Native* Worksheet (7) 'Ofcourses'
in which:	ofcourse Stan Ogden becomes an itinerant vicar, ofcourse Emily finally marries Digory Venn,
OR	ofcourse Emily does not marry Digoren Vig [whichever is the most inconsistent conclusion]
and	ofcourse Thomas Hardy finishes his brilliant sentence 'the wild, isolated changeable, unchangeable, Pagan, powerful, eggdon Heath . . .'

1 Has Thomas Hardy a 'lower moral quality' than a First Cause? (p. 387)
2 Is Clym Yeobright 'an unforeseen factor in the evolution of immortality'? (p. 387)
3 Compare the 'merrie England' exposition with the dramatic emphasis on Grandfer Cantle, (pp. 390 and 404). What are the differences?

4 What are the ironies Hardy is pointing to in Clym's reservations about Digory Venn? (pp. 399ff)
5 Clym walks the Heath during customary celebrations of vitality: Maypole and wedding songs. Why does Hardy have him wondering if the revellers think of him? (p. 410)
6 How does Hardy leave you feeling about Clym's preaching by his comments on p. 407 and the novel's final sentences?
7 Clym tells Thomasin that better husbands are found in towns (p. 399). Is this the stage to expect *Return of Return of the Native*?

TECHNIQUES CONSTRUCT MEANING

Students should have looked at the techniques used by a writer, not just so that they can refer to them to gain exam marks, but in order to understand the effect they have on a reader. The revision period is a time when this type of analysis should be assimilated by practice on key passages chosen by the student in support of her personal thesis.

LEARNING QUOTATIONS

Each individual will have selected key quotations from journals and essays in the process of developing the personal thesis. These will be brief (two lines or one sentence) and will need to be learned if the exam is not open-book. This process is often left too late. It is easier to revise learning of quotations if it has been seriously begun early on. Pinning up papers around the house so that you know where you're going to meet the one about . . . can be a good idea, saying it before you look at it, then checking and re-saying it while you're washing up or putting the kettle on! In addition, it is worthwhile learning one longer quotation from each text, especially from the long poem, if that is an element of the exam. Some points do need to be made about sequence, development, or patterning of meaning in a way that cannot be catered for by quoting two lines. One of us has tested each student for a ten-line correct quotation for *The Prelude*, at the end of lessons, only awarding a tick in the record when it has been correctly said and only receiving a tick himself when he's been able to do the same! A reminder that quotations should always be commented on may be necessary, and an essay point made by reference to the way language works in the quotation.

THE CRITICS

Reference has been made to learning two critical quotations for each text (and/or one statement by the writer). The selection of these statements should not be made on the basis of simple *support* for the student's thesis, but should be chosen in order to be qualified or argued with. This will have been the spirit of their collection in their journals in the latter stages of the course and the discipline of their use in essays. Staying consistent to the principle now will improve the writing of the exam answer.

A linguistic formula needs to be provided for introducing into the exam answer a point made by the unknown critic: a friend, a teacher, a forgotten writer. Some students will be aware that their own view differs from that expressed by someone else in the group or their teacher, and these are often good ways of making a personal position clear. So encouragement should be given to the use of a formula such as 'It can be argued that . . .' or 'Some readers might feel that . . .'

OPEN BOOKS

Some examinations of an open-book nature require clean texts but some, such as the JMB Syllabus C, allow for the personal marking of texts in order for candidates to find their way around them quickly. In these situations it is worth discussing the preparation of texts with the group so that overcrowding of the marks in the texts does not take place as anxiety mounts. Simple colour coding is better than anything else.

PLANNING ANSWERS

Some practice is needed in the breaking down of the parts of a question so that all its demands are covered, together with the construction of an argued answer that moves towards a thesis, defining its terms, establishing and qualifying its points along the way. A useful pattern of planning might be represented by this sequence:

Breakdown of question → spidergram(s) → list → argument → points and passages in final plan.

This needs practice without actually writing the essay so that it can be gradually brought down to ten minutes. It cannot be assumed that everyone can do this, simply because they will have to. Practice plans should be made to possible questions.

There is potential for group work here in inviting students to adopt the 'role of the expert' by saying what they, as examiners, are looking for in answer to questions and devising questions of a similar type, explaining to the rest of the class what they would expect in answers.

TIMED ESSAYS

Experience of writing essays, following the above planning practice, in exactly the actual time allowed in the exam is something which, again, needs gradual practice. In this way students will gain a sense of planning time and know how long it takes them to write a concluding paragraph summing up their argument and its stages or qualifications.

HANDLING PAST PAPERS

The students may well have been working for the last two years on the assumption that their course will form the entire contents of the examination paper. Actually handling past papers will not only defuse some of their shock value, but also enable them to find easily, within the pattern of the questions, the areas where their texts will appear or the sections that they need to answer.

TIMINGS WITHIN THE EXAMINATION PAPER

When the student enters the exam room on the day of the examination, she should know the exact time at which to move on to the next question or part of a question. In a complicated examination it is worth suggesting that students write down the actual times that they must move on as the first thing they do when they sit down. Again, prior discussion of this with the group avoids the false belief that over-running on the time allowed for an answer will gain more marks. We put it like this:

The highest marks are harder to get, will not be gained by longer answers, and the lowest marks on the next answer will be easier to get, so it is always more profitable to make yourself move on to the next answer exactly when the time comes round.

SOME FINAL EXAM TIPS FOR STUDENTS

1 Keep to the time limit on each question. Remember that the first marks are the easiest to get, and higher marks will not be gained by over-running your time limit.

2 Break down the questions into its parts. Proportion them. Select key quotes for each part.

3 Order your answer in paragraphs, planning your material. Make a thesis in your answer that makes it different from that of others.

4 Memorize *your* quotes for *your* points about the text, the parts about which *you* feel you have something strong to say.

5 Memorize many short quotes rather than long chunks (except for the long poem text if there is one), and key phrases that can be used within a sentence.

6 Use these quotations: make a general point, quote evidence, then comment on how the *language* in the quotation makes your point.

7 Say 'I think' directly and avoid pompous objectivity.

8 State alternative interpretations to your own and show their weaknesses, in the spirit of 'other readers might say . . .'

8

ALTERNATIVE A LEVELS

Of all candidates taking A level English Literature in 1985 10 per cent of candidates chose a syllabus which had an alternative element in it. This actually means that 5,767 candidates were experiencing some form of alternative to the traditional A level syllabus. Every board at present offers an alternative syllabus, with the exception of Northern Ireland, where it is under consideration. Very slowly, piecemeal, and in a remarkable variety of forms, the examination boards are experimenting with A level reform. Why is this happening? What common features are to be found in A level alternatives? Is the range of writing and reading really expanding for these candidates, or are teachers being given more freedom to teach new texts in the old ways with little real benefit to the experience of learners?

In the late 1970s the examination boards must have felt that the traditional security of A level English was being radically threatened by proposals for reform known as N and F. Supported by the Schools Council English 16–19 Project, which began work in 1975, the N and F proposed syllabus of 1977 made an attempt to define what might be included as content and/or activities in an English syllabus at A level. If N and F ultimately foundered it had asked some radical questions, revealed just how narrow traditional A level was, and posed a real if temporary threat, just at the time when another new approach to post-16 English in the form of the one-year course, CEE, was also newly posing an indirect threat to the traditional content and examining methods in English post-16 that A level represented. In 1976 the AEB published an alternative syllabus that offered an opportunity to any schools in the country which could form a viable regional group, a syllabus that was almost wholly different from the mainstream syllabus for A level English. Since 1969 JMB have offered Leicester schools an alternative syllabus, and since the late 1970s various boards have offered a variant examination to certain trusted public schools. But it has been the two threats of N and F and CEE which have prompted the boards actively to seek to develop reforms in experimental alternatives, perhaps with one eye to the market which would emerge from the increased take-up of coursework at 16-plus, now made compulsory in all GCSE syllabuses. When teachers have experienced the increased freedom, opportunities, and, dare one say, improved educational and examination results from coursework at GCSE, there may well emerge general dissatisfaction with even the present forms of Alternative A level syllabuses, as our final chapter suggests.

So what are the limitations of the traditional A level English Literature examinations and what are the features of the alternatives? The strengths and the weaknesses of traditional A level are associated with what has come to be regarded as the content and practice of English Literature study itself: practical criticism of a limited literary canon to the exclusion of other forms of writing by students and other forms of language use in our culture, assessed by the one-hour or less examination question. A recent HMI survey of A level English teaching in twenty comprehensive schools formulates its report in terms which point in the direction of features of alternative syllabuses:

> Several students had valued the personal writing which had characterized work in English in the first five years of secondary education and regretted that there were few occasions for it now. A large majority of students felt that an element of coursework assessment would be valuable and a common observation was that detailed set book study gave little time for wide personal reading.
>
> (HMI 1986: 2.5)

Here are three major features commonly to be found amongst the alternative syllabuses, apparently demanded by students themselves in conversations with HMI:

1 an element of coursework assessment;
2 a wider range of written work, including personal imaginative writing;
3 a wider range of reading, including personal choice.

If we add to this list open-book examinations and (rarely) oral assessment, we shall have represented all of the elements which might be drawn from different combinations to distinguish an alternative syllabus, although no two alternatives are exactly the same in their combination of elements or the proportion of marks given to those elements.

Let us consider in a little more detail some of the differences and the difficulties of these elements, drawing examples from the JMB Syllabus C because it is the one with which we are most familiar in detail.

Coursework

An element of coursework allows for some flexibility in the nature of the work, whether class or individual, whether on one or several texts, whether on traditional 'literary' texts or another genre such as journalism, perhaps even whether studies are made of written or of oral language use. Within a syllabus, variety of coursework within any of these choices might be demanded by the structure of the coursework element. The JMB A level Syllabus C, for example, demands one piece of personal imaginative writing and one piece on personal wide reading, but leaves optional the remaining components, requiring only that they represent study of different genre. Some boards require an extended essay in the coursework submitted, allowing the opportunity for the student to explore a theme or writer in some depth based on personal interest.

Differences exist most strikingly in the degree of teacher involvement in assessment. In some cases the external examiner makes a grade unaided by the school; in others the school offers its opinion and the examiner accepts or changes it; in others the teachers are involved in a series of agreement trials based on the 16-plus model, before offering their grades to the external examiner.

The difficulty with coursework in combination with examinations as a form of total assessment is largely a question of their interrelationship in terms of the proportions of the final grade and the status of the work. No board gives more than 50 per cent to the coursework element (Cambridge Syllabus 9000). The average is around one-third of the total. The status thus accorded to this valuable, varied, and student-oriented work is thus diminished by the examination-oriented work, which must dominate the course. What is the value of a 45-minute examination answer on a text in comparison with an extended essay on the same text? Coursework in its most imaginative and personalized form must make the dominant part of the assessment seem somewhat restricted.

In learning the skills of examination answers, students often find themselves unlearning other skills of writing that have been developed through earlier coursework.

A wider range of written work

When formulating their proposals for a Sheffield alternative syllabus to JMB (now Syllabus C), David Allen and Sue Horner (1980) noted that they sought a syllabus in which 'the candidate would be given credit for developing his own powers of written expression as well as for close and critical reading'. So this was to be a writing as well as a reading course, and one which saw the student as an art-producer as well as art-consumer. HMI have drawn attention to the disappointment of many students who lose the chance to develop what they have often been good at before starting A level: their own personal writing.

Many alternative A levels allow room for this in coursework but JMB Syllabus C, which the Sheffield alternative has become, remains the only one to *require* personal imaginative writing of some kind. This could be regarded as an indictment of how non–radical many alternatives may be in their practices. However, this may be unfair in that within the coursework submitted for other boards there may well be much writing that is different from the literary-critical essay so dominant in the examination. Directors' notebooks may represent the study of dramatic texts, and reflections on communism may be accepted if they take their starting-point in *Animal Farm*. Coursework can allow for the flexibility of placing such writing as is produced into different categories so that it is assessed by criteria appropriate to its form rather than its starting-point. In JMB Syllabus C, for example, a piece of writing which may have sprung from wide reading will be submitted under

'Composition' when it is the student's own exploration of an issue (for example, communication) rather than an account of the way an author explores it in a text (for example, *Animal Farm*). Such flexibility allows for the learning to take priority over the assessment process for a student and her writing.

The difficulties that are often seen here lie in the assessment of a wider range of writing than is found in the traditional A level. These difficulties appear to be sufficiently overcome at 16-plus for a range of writing to be *demanded* for assessment in GCSE coursework. The majority of candidates assessed by alternative schemes are taking part in nationally available schemes where boards seem satisfied that a wider range of writing can be assessed. Nevertheless, it must be said that teachers themselves within these schemes often express anxiety about grading imaginative writing in particular at this level.

Two points can be made to put this anxiety into perspective. First, these anxieties can be resolved only by practice in articulating the criteria of assessment for specific examples of work in relation to guidelines. 'What are the strengths and weaknesses of this poem and how do I balance their relevant importance in arriving at a grade, bearing in mind the potential achievements of this age group?' This is done at 16-plus and it is done for other forms of writing at A level. More practice in this is needed. Avoiding the issue will not resolve it, nor be doing students a service, if they're to be encouraged to be producers as well as consumers at A level.

Second, it may be helpful to students to develop a distinction between personal writing that remains personal, cathartic, and not intended for an audience other than the writer, and imaginative writing which attempts to communicate with a reader. Work which is submitted for assessment in a folder or selection of coursework must, by definition, be of the latter kind. As soon as work, even though it may have begun in the first category, is brought into the public domain it will be responded to (and in this case assessed) by its ability to communicate to a reader. This criterion was adopted from the start in the Sheffield alternative syllabus where the desire was to encourage experimentation, but ultimately within the disciplines of the concept of 'audience'. This does not, of course, mean that reaching agreement on grades is necessarily easier than with any other kind of writing, but it does place a rigorous discipline on the nervous preciousness that can suddenly descend upon the assessment of student poetry. If we are going to allow room for this important form of student writing on the course, as we should, it is important that these 'difficulties' are overcome in a practical manner.

A wider range of reading

One of the main reasons for teachers wanting A level reform has been a desire to choose the set texts themselves. This has not always been accompanied by a desire to provide students with the opportunity to be assessed on their own personal reading interests. However, it is by both of these means that the range of texts to be studied at A level has been expanded from the narrow Leavisite notion of 'the great tradition'. Free to choose some proportion of the set texts themselves, within either a coursework or examination paper context, or both, teachers have actually tended to reproduce traditional A level choices in much of their selection. There may be good reasons for this: Hardy, for example, raising tensions about position and passion in a way that is relevant and extending for class-conscious adolescents. But one question which should not be ignored is that of just how widely the teacher reads. How many A level teachers, for example, read plays or travel-writing with enough regularity to be able to recommend texts appropriate for students? It is noticeable that many of the recent novels which groups of teachers select are initially read as a result of cultural influences such as the Booker Prize publicity, appropriate though such novels may well turn out to be.

This question becomes important in relation to extending students' individual reading interests, in syllabuses where coursework has allowed for this to be represented. Some departments have regarded any staff as potential tutors for specific texts which students wish to discuss, treating the staff-room as a rich resource of reading interests. Some teachers may try to get students to develop a pattern of reading that explores a theme or a writer, focusing in a final discussion of two or three texts from the total list of books read. Some schools have a policy of deciding with the student an individual title or question to pursue through their writing, so that it has a sharply questioning focus as well as being a statement of personal interest and enjoyment.

Difficulties of assessment are sometimes raised again here,

following on from the difficulties of structuring guidance and writing on a wide range of texts. But again, working practice seems to produce a set of criteria that is acceptable to the major boards now assessing this kind of writing. Where the candidate assumes that the examiner has not read a book, sufficient evidence must be provided in the way it is described so that insights and impact can be assessed. Although writing about personal reading interests ought to be more subjective than examination essays, it will nevertheless be assessed by the candidate's public powers of expressing insights gained from the texts.

Open-book examinations

When students are allowed to take their set texts into the examination with them (open-book exams) new possibilities are opened for the nature of the questions set. Memory is less important and detailed reference may be made to the texture of the work itself. There is also a strong temptation for the candidate to spend too much time in searching rather than thinking and writing. But with preparation and practice this can be overcome, like any poor examination technique. Often the questions set do not in any way acknowledge that texts are available, the examiners presumably taking this into account in their grading.

Here are two questions set for an open-book examination in JMB's Syllabus C in 1987, the first of which is typical of those which utilize the availability of the text:

The Mill on the Floss: George Eliot

   a) What outstanding qualities do you find in Book III, Chapter 3 (The Family Council)? What function do you think this and similar episodes serve in the novel? Refer to one other comparable passage in your answer.

OR

   b) 'The story of wasted lives.' In what respects were Tom and Maggie Tulliver's lives wasted? What factors combined to bring about this waste?

The fact that these two quite different styles of question appear as alternatives in the same paper perhaps indicates a reluctance, even in the alternative syllabus to relinquish totally traditional styles of question, for example the given assumption of (b) and, inevitably, the traditional style of teaching that lies behind it. The first of these questions obviously needs different kinds of preparation and practice at using the text in this way with limited time, but it does assume an active reader who is directly addressed. The spirit is that of interest in a personal response. It is interesting to note that this type of question was first formulated by teachers in the Sheffield scheme and offered to the board as an example of the kind of question they would like to see in an open-book examination. This process of teachers offering guidance to a board is rare, and is ironic in that in the Sheffield proposals the board first wished to experiment with open-book questions against the initial wishes of the teachers (Allen and Horner 1980: 38).

Opinion on this form of examining remains divided. Dixon (1979: 162) regarded it as 'a possible opportunity to improve the quality of evidence available for "examination"'. Others might say that it is a minor reform, drawing attention away from the limitations of any 45-minute examination answer under the guise of answering the major criticism of memory testing. Whatever view is taken, it is becoming the dominant form of examining set texts in the Alternative A level syllabuses.

Oral assessment

Oral work has been pioneered at A level, if a little nervously, within the Cambridge 9000/10 Syllabus in which one-third of the total marks are allocated to a course devised by individual schools and approved by the board. It is, however, a very small number of schools that are awarding a proportion of grades for oral contributions in the course. Indeed the board's enthusiasm may be judged from the following guidance offered to schools: 'In order to avoid possible difficulties in these two areas – oral and creative work – we ask that schools anxious to include this type of work should confine themselves to only one of these elements.'

In practice schools adopt very different methods of assessing oral work. One school awards it 10 per cent of the marks for an upper sixth long study, which itself totals 50 per cent of the school-assessed marks. In this school an end-of-course grade is awarded for oral ability demonstrated in the ordinary process of discussing the long study with the tutoring teacher. Here the emphasis is on process, although the criteria for assessment might be a little undefined.

Another school awards 5 per cent of the total A level mark for oral performance in conducting a seminar in the final year, and for contributing to the seminars of others. The subject must be an integral part of the periods studied throughout the course, and the student will also submit a handout for the seminar together with an assessment of their own performance in leading the seminar. The two teachers present will submit a written comment on the seminar for the student's file, as will the other students present. Opportunity for the rehearsal of this experience is provided during the first year of the course. Here the emphasis is on a rigorous single assessment of oral ability by clearly identified criteria, at the expense of ignoring other speech situations.

Clearly there is plenty of room for further development here. Indeed, it would appear to be an urgent need that the boards, together with schools developing the nature of English at A level through alternative syllabuses, explore the possibilities for assessing what is obviously an essential element of the course at A level. The lessons being learnt in GCSE oral assessment will obviously be of benefit.

English Language A levels

In his National Association for the Teaching of English (NATE) publication on Alternative A levels, Bill Greenwell (1988) expresses the personal view that

> because English literature teachers have shied away for so long from the 'non-literary' – i.e. not-classic – use of language as legitimate material for inspection, analysis, stimulus, pleasure, they have been hijacked by a number of other syllabuses. . . . From my point of view, I think it's a pity that two English Language syllabuses have risen from, as I see it, the reluctance of English LITERATURE specialists to admit to being ENGLISH teachers.

Of course, many teachers would see AEB's Communication Studies A level and the detailed English Language A levels as offering wider opportunities for more studies of language usages than could possibly be incorporated into a single course of 'English' at A level. Certainly a look at the two English

Language syllabuses from JMB and London indicates the range and depth of work available to students.

Both rely on a final examination of theory and the study of specific examples of language usage. Both also require some form of personal project work on an aspect of contemporary written or spoken language. Both also allow for a taped presentation as part of this submission. Only the JMB syllabus requires the students to use language creatively for their own expression within the coursework. Here there is a stress on the need to produce drafts, commentaries, and reflections on the pieces written by the student. But the emphasis in these syllabuses is very much on technical analysis rather than evaluating meaning. And here is the crux of Bill Greenwell's reservations. Description and analysis in linguistic terms ought to be tools towards evaluation and engagement by students. It is not at all clear whether these two syllabuses go beyond the demand for the application of a body of knowledge derived from linguistics. In other words, the severance from literary or cultural studies' forms of practice looks to be complete, and divisively so, in these syllabuses. What has been gained, of course, is the opportunity to study and write diaries, documentaries, argument, songs, and manifestos, together with regional, social, and ethnic varieties of speech, if not culture.

Conclusions

It is significant that the demand from teachers for changes at A level, the patient persistence of schools or consortia who had formulated specific proposals, preceded the examination boards' cautious willingness to become more flexible in their notion of an A level course. On the surface, the current expansion of courses to include wider reading, creative writing, personal studies, even recognition of oral work, can be nothing but good, a widening of what counts as English post-16 to provide continuity with the English curriculum pre-16. Recognition needs to be given to the teachers who have led the boards in this direction by, in all cases, giving up extra time for the sake of better learning for their students.

Two reservations must remain, however. First, a student's *work* under an alternative syllabus need not necessarily be any different from that under the traditional A level. There may be more of it and it may be graded in a more complex way, but if the teacher chooses traditional texts and teaching methods a student can easily find that essays on set texts are little different from what she would have been reading and writing in following the traditional course. Unless, for example, creative writing is a compulsory element of the syllabus (as it is only in JMB Syllabus C) there is no necessity for teaching to develop creative language use. The literary critical essay may still be the exclusive mode of written expression in the course. Bill Greenwell, in the conclusions to his NATE survey of Alternative A levels, is particularly struck by this:

> I cannot understand why original personal writing is given such a hard time by some boards. . . . How come the UJEC and JMB can assess it, if it can't be assessed? We need to encourage the conscious ordering of original writing as a complement both to the study of language in use, and the language of different kinds of texts.
>
> (Greenwell 1988)

Similar arguments might be brought to bear on the inclusion of less traditional texts, non-literary texts, personal studies, language-in-use studies and oral assessment. 'Many of the "alternative" syllabuses', writes Bill Greenwell, 'are mutton dressed up as more palatable lamb'. A residual conservatism is inevitable from a total course structure which demands that the majority of marks are to be gained by performing the 45-minute critical essay in final examinations. It is from this starting-point that the second reservation about these 'alternative' syllabuses arises. An increasing number of teachers seem to be feeling that, despite some years of development now, there is little sign that the boards wish to follow through their discoveries in operating their A level syllabuses: that coursework works, that teachers on the whole like it, that a wider range of reading and writing can be assessed, and that all this leaves the final examinations as something of a contradictory enigma.

We seem to have come full circle, with a group of teachers demanding the reform of Alternative A levels. We refer back to Roy Goddard (1985) from the opening chapter of this book:

> But what might a radical alternative to A-level look like? On what rationale should it be based?

9
OTHER ALTERNATIVES?

How much longer can A level Literature remain cloistered in its belief in one infallible theory of reading, when there is overwhelming evidence that the study of literature is taking place in many different and exciting ways? We are not referring just to changes in literary fashion, but to deep divisions between theorists, critics, and teachers. Some concentrate on the author, some on the world represented, some purely on the text, some on the cultural context, some on the reader, some on language and some on the unconscious. Feminist critics challenge what they perceive as the patriarchal literary heritage and canon. Structuralists argue that meaning is determined by the relationships between structures that are habitually overlooked. Poststructuralists undermine earlier theories, questioning the basis of subjective experience by trying to demonstrate the instability of language and meaning.

We use shorthand terms in this brief summary of movements in critical theory, aware that many of the concerns are highly complex and inter-linked. It remains true, nevertheless, that A level remains cut off from many of these issues because it has hardly shifted ground since its inception in the 1930s. The continuing existence of the practical criticism paper is an annual homage to an analytical critical tradition developed in that period. Each year students are asked to comment on unseen verbal icons, seemingly uncontaminated by authorial, generic, historical, or cultural influences. Recent feminist writers have demonstrated how close reading by eminent critics can be radically challenged by adopting a different critical approach.

Isn't it time that traditions formed over two generations ago were reconsidered, particularly when the English curriculum below the sixth form has seen so many transformations? We have earlier referred to the random way the actual syllabuses at A level seem to be put together, with selection committees tinkering annually with a list of isolated texts. What other ways are there of designing syllabuses so that some of the fundamental questions about literature can be placed in the centre? For example:

1 What do we mean by literature? Which groups define it?
2 What are the differences between popular literature and other kinds? Have these differences always existed?
3 What do different readers value in literature? Why?
4 Who defines 'the literary heritage'? For what purposes?
5 What kind of help in our understanding and appreciation of a book do we want from the author, from scholars, reviewers, critics, and fellow readers?
6 Do we think that a text can be fully explicated and revealed?
7 What is meant by the writer's cultural context? How do we go about reconstructing it?

These are some of the issues that one group of A level teachers wanted to explore with their students, but any other group could produce a similar list. Questions of this kind cannot be discussed unless students are given access to a wider range of literature than that enshrined in the A level book lists. Not all books have to be studied in depth, if students are shown different ways of approaching certain genres or modes. But it seems to us essential that they are introduced to works by contemporary writers as well as established classics.

Students' understanding of what we mean by literature can be enhanced by their perceptions about the publication and reception of a recent book. How have their perceptions been mediated? What has been the influence of reviews, articles, media programmes? If the author has been interviewed, or invited to comment on his or her new work, what have these comments contributed to the student reader's awareness of context? How does this publication compare to one in the 1920s, say, or 1850s, or late eighteenth century? How do we find out? How does this particular text relate to earlier ones by the author, and to other texts within that genre? In other words, students will be learning about how certain kinds of knowledge are constructed, and by whom.

If students gain insights into how their accumulating knowledge of contemporary literature and culture is being constructed and mediated, they should be better prepared to investigate the pluralist interpretations of books from other periods. They will be warned against expectations of stable, fixed knowledge, although this is just what many of the literary histories and handbooks seem to provide. Where have our perceptions about the past come from? What artists, historians, and critics have contributed to our images of culture, of England, of poetry, and so on?

If this kind of inquiry were introduced it would surely banish forever such A level questions as the following:

'Donne is a scholar, not a poet.' Discuss.

The definitions of scholar and poet in the seventeenth century and in our own time differ so much as to render the statement meaningless. It could tell us something about attitudes to poetry at a certain period of history, but typical of so many citations in A level questions, it is anonymous and undated. Nevertheless, it is offered in inverted commas as the voice of authority.

But there are other reasons for including contemporary literature. Students in the sixth form will be trying to cope with views of life and society thrust at them by the media, by politicians, by financial experts, by military leaders and so on. What have living artists to say about life in the final years of this century? Do writers appear to offer alternative visions of society, perhaps in the form of a utopia, or by re-creating a 'golden age'? Is the writer sympathetic to the world as he sees it, or hostile? What aspects of life does he or she value, or place hope in? Do readers recognize a representation of the world they inhabit? What help do students need in trying to understand the books of living writers? Some teachers may argue that there should be an option in contemporary literature, as there is for twentieth-century literature in some syllabuses, but this is not the place to discuss details of that kind.

Not least of the reasons for including recent literature is that the student will find a wide variety of genres and forms to choose from for her own writing. Every year keen students of English are disappointed and frustrated when they discover that an advanced course in reading and writing restricts them almost exclusively to the critical essay. Even the long study or extended essays in some alternative syllabuses do not compare favourably with the major opportunities to produce a project (30 per cent of the course) in A level 'Communication Studies'. If we want to help students to develop as thinkers and writers, shouldn't we consider all forms of linguistic production, both 'creative' and instrumental? Options could be offered in many forms – autobiography, oral history and biography, short story, drama, poetry, radio or television script, and so on. These are not new proposals, of course, but they seem to get little public discussion. Is that because A level is for a minority of pupils and not in the mainstream of the English curriculum?

The range of written forms is directly related to the variety of reading which could be introduced at A level. We are not in the business of designing a new A level, but we would like to conclude with some suggestions. Is there a place for genre studies at A level, including some of the popular genres, such as science fiction or the thriller? *Brave New World*, *Island*, and *Nineteen Eighty Four* have appeared, but no titles from feminist science fiction. Autobiographical novels are often included, and autobiography as an option has great potential for students' writing, and there are many new publications, especially by women writers, of outstanding quality and interest.

If period studies are to be opened out, who defines the period and its representation? Is a decade a useful label for a period, or should other possibilities be considered (for example the age of Shakespeare, the Jazz age, and so on)? Why can't more popular or minority forms of writing be included in period studies, for example mass observation, and novels by working-class writers, in the 1930s? In any study of the First World War, there are now more diaries and accounts by ordinary soldiers and also collections of women's poetry (see Virago publications) to place against the more familiar works by officer poets.

Thematic options are rare at A level, although many questions are directed towards a consideration of themes, and some writers seem to foreground certain themes. One way to design a syllabus might be to collect texts around a theme, for example images of rural (or urban) England as represented in selected poems, novels, autobiographies, and oral histories; parent–child relationships; class issues. By isolating one issue there is always the danger of distorting a whole text, but that kind of problem itself should be part of the agenda on any advanced course in reading. Other possibilities might be to merge generic and thematic options; for example images of rural England in narrative poems, or short stories.

We have not yet referred to other options, in particular language and cultural studies, which many teachers regard as important new directions. Both labels can be used for separate A levels (see Chapter 8), or as a way of integrating studies, allowing different approaches. Thus images of rural England might be considered more broadly under cultural studies, to include photography and landscape painting, and an autobiographical option could include work on the different languages in oral histories and in written diaries and journals. Options like this offer wider perspectives on literature and society and also allow experimental forms of presentation; for example, a group exhibition of images of England, including detailed comments on literary extracts, photographs and illustrations. With generously defined coursework elements, this kind of work could count towards final assessments.

The debate about the proportion of coursework available at A level is bound to be influenced by developments in GCSE. But there is another issue which needs urgent attention. If examinations are to be retained for literature, then we should urgently consider which kinds of examination tasks are most suitable, in the light of recent research. Is the unseen question on a complete text really defensible? Are there alternatives to the practical criticism paper? Are open-book exams (with suitably worded questions) the best way forward? Can A level boards learn from some of the interesting changes in forms of examination in higher education? We have no doubts about the need for reforms in examining literature. Reading examiners' reports over the past decade only confirms and strengthens our belief: there are so many complaints about 'mechanical', tired writings, as if only the students were to blame and not the system.

This leads to our final point. If A level is to be relevant for all those students who want to read and write at an advanced level, more consideration should be given to them both as readers and producers. That means designing real syllabuses, not just providing a list of books. It does not mean choosing less demanding books, but it should enable students to study culture and society in their own time, as well as in the past, and it should given them a wide range of opportunities to report on their own experience of life and literature. The alternative syllabuses have made a brave start, but all teachers who are dissatisfied with the existing orthodoxy need to make their voices heard.

There are teacher representatives on all the English committees or panels of the examination boards, and many of these teachers are members of NATE. There are also examiners and moderators to write to, or to invite to local meetings. Examination reform is slow and it makes great demands on teachers' stamina and patience, but what has already been achieved provides a hopeful springboard for further more radical changes.

BIBLIOGRAPHY

General references

Adams, A. and Hopkins, T. (eds) (1981) *Sixth Sense*, Glasgow: Blackie.

Allen, D. and Horner, S. (1980) 'A new A level syllabus', *English in Education* 14, 2: 36–42.

Barnes, D. and Barnes, D. (1984) *Versions of English*, London: Heinemann.

Blatchford, R. (ed.) (1986) *The English Teacher's Handbook*, London: Hutchinson.

Cosway, P. (1987) 'A plea for a multi-ethnic approach to A level English', *English in Education* 21, 3: 50–5.

Daw, P. (1986) 'There is an alternative', *English in Education* 20, 2: 62–71.

Dixon, J. (1979) *Education 16–19: The Role of English and Communication*, London: Macmillan.

Dixon, J. and Brown, J. (1984) *Responses to Literature – What is Being Assessed?*, London: Schools Council.

Fry, D. (1981) 'Reflecting on English: keeping work diaries', in M. Torbe (ed.) *Language, Teaching and Learning*, London: Ward Lock Educational.

Gifford, T. and Brown, J. (1983) 'Creative responses in the sixth form', in B. Harrison (ed.) *English Studies 11–18: An Arts-Based Approach*, London: Hodder & Stoughton.

Goddard, R. (1985) 'Beyond the literary heritage: meeting the needs in English at 16–19', *English in Education* 19, 2: 12–22.

Greenwell, B. (1988) *Alternatives at English A Level*, Sheffield: National Association for the Teaching of English.

HMI (1986) *A Survey of the Teaching of A Level English Literature in Twenty Mixed Sixth Forms in Comprehensive Schools*, London: DES.

Jackson, D. (1983) *Encounter with Books*, London: Methuen.

Jackson, D. and Brown, J. (eds) (1984) *Varieties of Writing*, London: Macmillan.

NATE (1988) *English A Level in Practice*, NATE Post-14 Committee, Sheffield: National Association for the Teaching of English.

Newbolt Report (1921) *The Teaching of English in England*, London: HMSO.

Ogborn, J. (1984) 'Teaching A level: a two-year plan', *English Magazine* 12: 15–20.

Peim, N. (1986) 'Redefining A level', *English Magazine* 17: 10–17.

Protherough, R. (ed.) (1986) *Teaching Literature for Examinations*, Milton Keynes: Open University Press.

Schools Council (1979) *The Effective Use of Reading*, London: Heinemann.

Stanton, M. (1980) 'Art exists to make the stone storey', *English in Education* 14, 3: 42–55.

Stevens, F. (1970) *English and Examination*, London: Hutchinson.

Shakespeare

Adams, R. (ed.) (1985) *Teaching Shakespeare*, London: Robert Royce.

Berry, R. (ed.) (1976) *On Directing Shakespeare*, London: Croom Helm.

Bradley, A.C. (1904) *Shakespearean Tragedy*, London: Macmillan.

Davison, P. (1983) *Hamlet*, Text and Performance series, London: Macmillan.

Dollimore, J. (1982) *Radical Tragedy*, Brighton: Harvester.

Dollimore, J. and Sinfield, A. (1985) *Political Shakespeare*, Manchester University Press.

Greer, G. (1986) *Shakespeare*, Oxford University Press.

Hunt, A. (1974) *Arden*, London: Methuen.

Kitto, H.D.F. (1959) *Form and Meaning in Greek Drama*, London: Methuen.

Knight, G. Wilson (1949) *The Wheel of Fire*, London: Methuen.

Kott, J. (1964) *Shakespeare Our Contemporary*, London: Methuen.

Lawrence, D.H. (1916) *Twilight in Italy*, Harmondsworth: Penguin.

Miller, J. (1986) *Subsequent Performances*, London: Faber.

New Swan Shakespeare (1969) *Hamlet*, London: Longman.

Open University Unit (1971) *Hamlet*, Milton Keynes: Open University Press.

Pafford, M. (1985) 'Shakespeare rules OK', *The Use of English* 36, 3: 49–52.

Shakespeare on Stage (1984) Cambridge: Cambridge Educational Press.

Sher, A. (1985) *Year of the King*, London: Methuen.

Showalter, E. (1985) 'Representing Ophelia: women, madness and the responsibilities of feminist criticism', in P. Parker and G. Hartman (eds) *Shakespeare and the Question of Theory*, London: Methuen.

Styan, J.L. (1977) *The Shakespeare Revolution*, Cambridge University Press.

Tillyard, E.M.W. (1943) *The Elizabethan World Picture*, London: Chatto & Windus.

Literary criticism and theory

Abel, E. (ed.) (1982) *Writing and Sexual Difference*, Brighton: Harvester.

Belsey, C. (1980) *Critical Practice*, London: Methuen.

Bennett, T. (1979) *Formalism and Marxism*, London: Methuen.

Booth, W. (1961) *The Rhetoric of Fiction*, Chicago, Ill: Chicago University Press.

Culler, J. (1975) *Structuralist Poetics*, London: Routledge & Kegan Paul.

Donovan, J. (1975) *Feminist Literary Criticism*, Lexington, Ky: Kentucky University Press.

Eagleton, T. (1978) *Criticism and Ideology*, London: Verso.

—— (1983) *Literary Theory: An Introduction*, Oxford: Blackwell.

Eco, U. (1979) *The Role of the Reader*, Bloomington, Ill. and London: Indiana University Press.

Fish, S. (1980) *Is there a Text in this Class?*, Cambridge, Mass: Harvard University Press.

Hobsbaum, P. (1970) *A Theory of Communication*, London: Macmillan.

Iser, W. (1978) *The Art of Reading*, Baltimore, Md: Johns Hopkins University Press.

Jefferson, A. and Robey, D. (eds) (1986) *Modern Literary Theory*, London: Batsford.

Kermode, F. (1983) *Essays on Fiction*, London: Routledge & Kegan Paul.

Leavis, F.R. (1948) *Education and the University*, London: Chatto & Windus.

——— (1979) *Reading Out Poetry* lecture, Queen's University of Belfast.

Lowenthal, D. (1985) *The Past is a Foreign Country*, Cambridge University Press.

Millett, K. (1977) *Sexual Politics*, London: Virago.

Moffett, J. (1986) *Teaching the Universe of Discourse*, Boston, Mass: Houghton Mifflin.

——— (1981) *Active Voice*, New Jersey: Boynton, Cook.

Potter, S. (1937) *The Muse in Chains*, London: Cape.

Richards, I.A. (1929) *Practical Criticism*, London: Routledge & Kegan Paul.

Rosenblatt, L. (1978) *The Reader, the Text, the Poem*, Bloomington, Ill: Southern Illinois University Press.

Scholes, R. (1979) *Structuralism in Literature*, New Haven, Conn: Yale University Press.

Selden, R. (1985) *A Reader's Guide to Contemporary Literary Theory*, Brighton: Harvester.

Tallack, D. (ed.) (1987) *Literary Theory at Work*, London: Batsford.

Tompkins, J.P. (ed.) (1980) *Reader-Response Criticism*, Baltimore, Md: Johns Hopkins University Press.

Williams, R. (1983) *Writing in Society*, London: Verso.